for my Mother

John Amor

13th December 2010

ibis initiation time

john houston

the scots philosopher and mystic

Published by

MELROSE BOOKS

An Imprint of Melrose Press Limited
St Thomas Place, Ely
Cambridgeshire
CB7 4GG, UK
www.melrosebooks.com

FIRST EDITION

Copyright © John Houston 2010

The Author asserts his moral right to
be identified as the author of this work

Cover designed by John Houston

ISBN 978 1 907040 54 2

Printed and bound in Great Britain by:
CPI Antony Rowe. Chippenham, Wiltshire

FSC
www.fsc.org
MIX
Paper from
responsible sources
FSC® C013604

Contents

Dedicated to the appearance of the School of Philosophy along Platonic lines advocated by George Gemistos Plethon and mentioned to Cosimo de' Medici at the time of *The Council of Florence* in 1439.

Foreword

At the time of Great Transition, such as these days in which we live, when there is so much uncertainty as to the direction the Human Race should pursue, it is then that the Word of God *comes* to us. Prophetic insight is a *Divine Provision*.

From the Old Testament we see that the Word of God *came* to Isaiah; the Word of God came to Jeremiah; the Word of God also came to Ezekiel; furthermore, the Word of God came to Jonah "a second time".

From the New Testament we have narratives referring to Jesus of Nazareth. We are informed that He is the embodiment of the Word of God which "had been made flesh and dwelt amongst us". He is portrayed as the One who *reveals* the Word of God to us and yet there is more; the Word of God is actually a Person and *He* is that Person.

When Jesus of Nazareth is depicted as starting out on what was His Divine Mission on Earth, He goes to where those *destined* to be His disciples are to be found. They did not find Him. He went *to* them. He introduces Himself to them where they are and *as* they are in their everyday, mundane circumstances. He went to where *they* were.

This is only possible because of the Process of Incarnation. But who is this who has appeared to us in Human form or *as* a Human being? From the New Testament, we see the scene where Jesus is being baptised. A voice is heard from Heaven, which is *another* world. Something or someone from that other world was seen to transcend this world *through* Jesus of Nazareth.

The message of the New Testament is that Beings from another world, the world of the Biblical Angels, are intent upon reproducing themselves here, *through* us. They have created the circumstances which permit *them* to reproduce themselves *here* through us. This is what the evolution of Human culture is actually about. This is its true purpose. This is why we are *as* we are.

The message of the New Testament is that there is a Prince from another world to whom the planet Earth *belongs* as an inheritance. Somehow or other the Prince must prove Himself to be worthy of His inheritance.

A Celestial Marriage is taking place. Heaven and Earth are being united by means of the Human Race. Such is the Esoteric Truth concerning the Pyramids of Egypt because Old Heaven was trying to reproduce Itself here on Earth. The Pyramids symbolised the marriage of the Earth with Sirius, heralding the advent of *God-like* qualities in Human beings.

The message of the New Testament is that a Cosmic Being has been *incarnated* here, and will be *again*. Jesus of Nazareth is depicted as having *assumed* Human form for the sake of Incarnation.

The Incarnation on Earth of the Son of God or, if you prefer, the Supreme Personality of Godhead means that there will no longer be a barrier in terms of Consciousness between the Earth and Sirius. Cosmic Consciousness is now possible for the Human Race as this Cosmic Being is actually *activating* our Racial Memory.

The Universal Self of everything that exists has emanated from an Archetypal Image in the Mind of the Original Godhead, also known as the Ultimate Ancestor.

It is because of the Incarnation of a Cosmic being on Earth that we have been able to become more conscious, more evolved and civilised and through us there is a Regaining, a Rebirth, a Recollection of the Original Consciousness. This Regaining of Consciousness is the *Manifestation* of the Supreme Personality of Godhead at one level; on another level it is the *Rebirth* of Humanity.

In the Hermetic Tradition, also known as *The Corpus Hermeticum*, we read of the Mind Shepherds and that they are "the Logos of God". It is interesting indeed to note that they are referred to as "the Logos" as well as being Mind Shepherds.

The Logos is the means whereby the Cosmos is guided *out* of Chaos and *towards* Order. None other than the Creative Principle of the Universe is at work here. The Mind Shepherds are described as operating towards the fulfilment of their task to unite all worlds, with worlds as aspects of *Mind*.

By means of the Human Race a *Necessary Being* is being created. This is a Necessary Self-Evolving Being which can meet *all* the requirements for the *Manifestation* of the Ultimate Ancestor. Thereby, that which is *manifested* is, quite simply, the Predisposition of the Ultimate Ancestor to *become* the Supreme Personality of Godhead.

Through Incarnation, the Ultimate Ancestor can *reveal* Itself on Earth and through the Human Race It is able to reproduce Itself as a Collective Consciousness. The Purpose of Life is that the Original Archetype, who became the Ultimate Ancestor, may be able to reproduce Itself as a Collective Consciousness.

Here we have to consider the Ultimate Ancestor and Its nature: 'In the beginning' there was Predisposition. This Predisposition was the source of a Process of Personalisation for the sake of the Acquisition of Identity. This was in order that the Predisposition to *be* God would be able to manifest Itself.

The Quest appears as the need for the Acquisition of Identity and so it is; but It seeks a special Identity for the Identity is required for the Purpose of Incarnation.

Not even an Omnipotent Being can come into existence fully developed. It is Predisposition which is being reproduced and necessarily so since Predisposition is *all* there is.

The Ultimate Ancestor was able to begin a Process of Personalisation for the sake of the Acquisition of Identity, being the means of expression for the Archetypal Image. As it happens, this Archetype emanated from the Self-Experience of the Predisposition to *be* God.

The Archetype was aware that this was happening because the Archetype made the *self-experience* of such Predisposition *possible*. It was a reaction to It. Now that self-experience of It is that which the Ultimate Ancestor seeks to express and reproduce.

For the Ultimate Ancestor, the task is Reproduction which is only possible when that Archetypal Pattern is made manifest *for* Reproduction. The Archetypal pattern appears amongst us as the Christ, the Son of God, as Ion, the Son of Apollo, as Krishna or as Hermes Trismegistus.

For the Reproduction of the Archetype and, thereby, the Predisposition which gains Self-Expression in this manner demands the *Incarnation* of the Archetype in order that others may be reproduced and the Archetype may become a Collective Consciousness.

This is where the Human Race comes in because our Ultimate Ancestor in being able to *assume* Human Form is able, at the same time, to Incarnate for the sake of Reproduction.

The Ultimate Ancestor requires this. *If* the Ultimate Ancestor is to become the Supreme Personality of Godhead then it is *dependent* upon the existence of the *Relationship of Godhead*. Without the *Relationship* of Godhead the Ultimate Ancestor cannot be the Supreme Personality of Godhead.

If the Ultimate Ancestor can become Many from being originally One then the Relationship of Godhead can go on forever; thus the need for a Necessary Self-Evolving Being.

The Ultimate Ancestor had to *change* to forsake being One to become Many; the Incarnation makes such change possible.

Incarnation is the good end of the Predisposition which makes everything possible. The Quest for Identity is the Process of the Self-Expression of Predisposition.

The task is for the One to reproduce Itself as a Collective Consciousness, as a Relationship of Godhead, the entities all limited and imperfect sharings of the Same Idea, the Idea whose Predisposition is the Predisposition to *be* God, or to *become* God.

If the Hermetic Tradition, which is the *undercurrent* of the Western Philosophical Tradition, is correct then the implication is that, *before* anything else can happen relating to entering a New Age, or relating to the experience of an Awakening of the Human Race *to* a higher level of Consciousness than we can *presently* appreciate, then Hermes Trismegistus *must* make an appearance.

This is *a necessity* for Hermes; it is also a necessity for us for we are dependent upon Hermes for further guidance in the process of our *Deification*.

Should Hermes Trismegistus make an appearance amongst us what should we expect? What sort of fellow might He be? Would He have a nice smile and broad shoulders? What about good teeth?

If this is the manifestation of *The Limit* spoken of by Pythagoras, *The Limit* who is the One who contains and provides an Identity conducive to the manifestation of *The Unlimited*, then we will witness *The Infinite* at work, and *The Infinite* will be *playing the part* of a Human being.

In seeing Hermes Trismegistus, the Son of God and *The Messenger of the gods*, indeed the Supreme Personality of Godhead, we will see the like of which we would never have dreamt possible.

When we hear Him speak or make Music we will know for certain that although we would have thought it unbelievable that One such as this *could* exist, nonetheless, He is here amongst us.

One glimpse will be enough to alter the course of Human history. Being perfectly proportioned, His beauty will be overpowering. No one will be able to look away for He is beyond comparison.

Wheeler emphasised that science had many mysteries left to explain.

"We live still in the childhood of Mankind," he said. "All these horizons are beginning to light up in our day: molecular biology, DNA, cosmology. We're just children looking for answers."

He served up another aphorism: as the island of our knowledge grows so does the shoreline of our ignorance.

Yet he was also convinced that Humans would someday find *The Answer*. In search of a quotation that expressed his faith, he jumped up and pulled down a book on information theory and physics to which he had contributed an essay. After flipping it open, he read:

"Surely someday, we can believe, we will grasp the central idea of it all as so simple, so beautiful, so compelling that we will all say to each other, 'Oh, how could it have been otherwise! How could we all have been so blind for so long!'."

Wheeler looked up from the book; his expression was beatific.

"I don't know whether it will be a year or a decade, but I think we can and will understand. That's the central thing I would like to stand for. We can and will understand."

Many modern scientists, Wheeler noted, shared his faith that Humans would one day find *The Answer*. For example, Kurt Godel, once Wheeler's neighbour in Princeton, believed that *The Answer* might *already* have been discovered.

He thought that maybe among the papers of Leibniz, which in his time had not been fully smoked out, we would find the... what was the word?... the philosopher's key, the magic way to find truth and solve any set of puzzlements.

Godel felt that this key "would give a person who understood it such power that you could only entrust the knowledge of this philosopher's key to people of high moral character".

John Horgan, *The End of Science*
Published in the USA by Addison-Wesley in 1996
Published in the UK by Little, Brown & Company in 1997
From the essay, *The End of Physics*, page 83

1: Renaissance Completion

What we refer to as *The Renaissance* which began in Florence in the fifteenth century was only an *interim stage* in a process which is now due to *fully* take place; this will *completely* alter life on Earth for everyone, *for ever*.

In the fifteenth century there was great change and progress did take place. This would pave the way for the Reformation which would see the advent of the British Empire which was built upon the English language and upon Protestantism.

In fifteenth century Florence, under the guidance of *George Gemistos Plethon*, influence was exerted to see a process which saw a fresh interest in Plato, whom Plethon considered to be the greatest philosopher of all. Plethon had put it into the mind of Cosimo de' Medici to see the appearance of a School of Philosophy along *Platonic* lines (1).

George Gemistos Plethon had hoped to see Plato recognised as the greatest philosopher of all, as the *philosophus maximus*; but he wanted more.

He had also hoped to see the foundation of a New Religion which looked to *Zoroaster* as its greatest inspiration and which, essentially, would be Sun-worship. Yet it would not stop there for he wanted to see both Jesus Christ and the prophet Muhammed *not only replaced but forgotten*, and he stated that the time would come when this would happen.

To whom could he have been referring who would be able to replace both Jesus Christ and the prophet Muhammed? By means of prophetic insight, could he have been referring to something that happened in Rome in 1481 and then in 1484 when, as has been alleged, there was the *miraculous* appearance of

1

an Angel of Divine Wisdom, the latest *manifestation* of Hermes Trismegistus (2), one known as *Giovanni Mercurio da Correggio*?

Plethon would be disappointed for he had been seeing "as through a glass darkly". Plato did not emerge as *philosophus maximus*, and neither were both Muhammed and Jesus Christ replaced, as he had hoped. Neither was there the establishment of his New Religion, based on Traditions which went back to Zoroaster and which was essentially Sun-worship.

The world was not yet ready for that message. The lines of communication were not open on a global scale; *but they are now.* The time has now arrived for the culmination of many millions of years of *genetic engineering*. We shall see *The Promised One*, the coming of whom *Religions have foretold* and whom we all anticipate. The Great Shepherd, the One who has guided the Human Race this far, will have returned and been *revealed* to us.

This Person, the Great Shepherd, has come to the Earth to *rule*, to see the establishing of a Kingdom which will continue "until times indefinite".

Our Ultimate Ancestor, in coming to Earth, has actually journeyed *into Pre-Existence* where the only Reality is *Pre-disposition* so that our Ultimate Ancestor may be able to *reproduce* Itself. In the reproduction of sub-personalities our Ultimate Ancestor is able to reproduce Itself *as a Collective Consciousness* as the only way to interact with Itself, as It and *only* It actually exists.

With the *manifestation* of the Ultimate Ancestor to *rule* on Earth, this will herald the *end* of the *Human stage* of our evolution as we have known it. By this means, a new Humanity will appear, a Humanity the fruits of whom will be able to be *fully assimilated* into the Godhead.

Here we see the *purpose* of the Human Race, to render possible the *assimilation* of the purest *Reproductions* of the Ultimate Ancestor into the Godhead so that *the Divine Identity*, as a Collective Consciousness, may be complete.

This is what is going to happen on Earth: but what is going to happen as from now? How will we arrive at this situation?

We are now in the cusp between two Ages. As things are, we will not see the full dawning of the New Age until 2242 AD, with the beginning of what is known as *The Age of Saturn* (3).

There will be a process of stabilisation on Earth; fundamental to this will be the appearance of the *Kingdom of God*, this Kingdom being built upon the political and economic union of the English-speaking nations, with others.

2

The establishing of this Kingdom will, in effect, constitute *the resurrection of the British Empire.*

This Kingdom will be built upon the English-language and will go *beyond* Protestantism to the appearance of *The True Religion* of the Human Race. Within this Kingdom, the Scots will be the Royal Nation, with the Scots ruling on Earth by the grace of God.

In the Bible, in *The Second Book of Kings* (4), we read that there will be *three* overturnings. Esoteric Tradition informs us that *two* have already happened; the first was around 500 AD when the Scots established their colony of *Dal Riada* in what would become known as Scotland; the second was in 1603 when James VI, King of Scots, became James I, King of Great Britain and Ireland. Then the British Empire began, leading to the scattering of the royal Scottish seed throughout the world.

According to Esoteric Tradition there is one overturning to come. This will be the Ultimate Ancestor emerging to rule the world. Just as the King of Scots ruled the British Union at the dawn of the British Empire so the King of Scots should rule at the *resurrection* of the British Empire. This time the sovereignty of the King of Scots will be *global* in extent. Ancient prophecy will then be fulfilled.

What of this *True Religion* of which the Ancient Scots became the supreme custodians? The True Religion, the True Christianity if you will, was *not* built upon Jesus Christ but upon *Ion*, the Son of Apollo. This is why Saint Columba (5), founded a community in what was to become known as *Scotland*, the island upon which it was built would become known as *Iona*, in honour of *Ion.*

So a Kingdom will emerge in accordance with the will of God. Its King will be none other than Ion, the Son of Apollo, a fabulous musician and one who is incredibly beautiful, as the *express image* of the Heavenly Father.

NOTES

(1) The Medici family would befriend Plethon and, in addition to this, the Medici family would receive instruction from Plethon in matters pertaining to Astrology.

(2)   Belief in *The Messenger of the gods* was ancient as well as widespread and *not* restricted to the early Christians, for there is *nothing unique* about the Christian message.

(3)   Nostrodamus stated in connection with his writings that "these are perpetual prophecies until the year 3797". This is an *encoded* date. If we take 3797 and subtract the date of writing, which was 1555, we are left with 2242, being 3797 minus 1555.

In 2242 AD the Rulership of the Sun gives way to the Rulership of Saturn. The purpose of this book is *not* Astrology; however, Nostrodamus was referring to a 354-year cycle, which exists among other cycles such as a 504-year cycle and a 2160-year cycle, to name but two.

The Rulership of *Venus* began in 1180, the Rulership of the *Moon* in 1534, the Rulership of the *Sun* in 1888 and the Rulership of *Saturn* in 2242 AD.

People are also intrigued by what is often referred to as "the dawning of the Age of Aquarius" which is of a different order from the (what for us is the) *chronological* passage evident to those who have a keen interest in Astrology and are familiar with the Zodiacal Cycle. When we are referring to Ages which last for 2160 years the passage is different indeed.

Under normal circumstances the zodiacal cycle begins with Aries and continues with Taurus, Gemini, Cancer, Leo, Virgo, Libra, Scorpio, Sagittarius, Capricorn, Aquarius and, latterly, Pisces. As we see from this sequence, Pisces follows *after* Aquarius.

With the dawning of *The Age of Aquarius* we see that the cycle mentioned above is altered for here the trend is *reversed* because Aquarius now follows Pisces, denoting a process in *reverse*.

This will mean that *The Age of Aquarius* could fully begin around 2160 years after 70 AD, or 2230 AD; but Aquarius will *not* appear as such for Pisces will *disappear*. Pisces will be stripped away like the peeling of an onion. The Piscean layer will be stripped away to leave Aquarius, like a snake shedding skin.

Before the dawning of Aquarius there will be a period of *overlap* or dual-influence brought about by a cusp; as it happens, a cusp projects into both Ages by about 3.5 degrees, with one degree in terms of the process of equinoxes being about 70 years.

(4) See *The Second Book of Kings*, chapter 25.7. This is part of the Old Testament.

The Esoteric Tradition mentioned here does not have its basis in Biblical Literalism but in a Tradition which was the undercurrent of the Western Philosophical Tradition.

(5) Saint Columba, or Colm Cille, emanated from those who were the most powerful kindred in Ireland. These were known as the *Ui Neill*. Their descendants have surnames such as Gallagher, Docherty and Boyle.

There is a Tradition that Colm Cille presided over the coronation of Aedan Mac Gabrain, Kind of Dal Riada, in 574 AD; this could be described as the first Christian coronation in Europe.

Colm Cille belonged to a Tradition which asserted that *ogam* was the Gaidhlig (Gaelic) equivalent of the Roman alphabet.

It was maintained that Gaidhlig had been created after the Biblical Fall of the Tower of Babel.

2: Royal Lie/Secret Doctrine

I

From immemorial Antiquity there has always been the belief that there has existed a *Body of Wisdom* which was passed on *orally* and in *secret* from initiate to initiate and in the growth of Human Civilisation there are many who have lived their lives in the hope of uncovering this *Wisdom*.

Such people gave up everything in life in order to completely dedicate themselves to the acquisition of *Ancient Wisdom* and to the attainment of this Sacred and Secret Knowledge and, within living memory, there are some from whom we can gain insight.

One such person was H.P. Blavatsky who is recognised as having clearly studied and highly revered the Teachings of the Tibetan Lamas. In addition to this, it is accepted that she had continual contact with Sufis, with this having determined her world view and Teaching Methods.

We know that in 1878 she wrote to Professor Hiram Corson; in the letter she stated that she belonged to a *secret* sect of the Druzes of Mount Lebanon and that she lived her life among Dervishes, Persian Mullahs and Mystics of every description.

She was to travel to Tibet, going from Turkey in 1868 after which she returned to Egypt in 1871. In the early days of *The Theosophical Society* it was directed by 'the Egyptian Brotherhood at Luxor' (1).

In 1875, in an article entitled *The Science of Magick* for the magazine *The Spiritual Scientist*, she wrote of the Brotherhood at Luxor, stating that it was a section of the Grand Lodge of which she was a member. Mention was also made of Lahore, known for centuries as a centre for Sufi activity, where there were Sufi fraternities such as the Naqshbandi, Qadiri and Chishti Orders (2).

Her most direct reference to Sufism and to her search for Ancient Wisdom appears in an article published posthumously and entitled *The Eastern Gupta Vidya and the Kaballah* (3). In it she stated:

> This makes it plain that the Kaballah of the Jews is but a distorted echo of *The Secret Doctrine of the Chaldeans*, and the real Kaballah is found only in *The Chaldean Book of Numbers* now in the possession of some Persian Sufis.

This *Chaldean Book of Numbers* is cited frequently in *The Secret Doctrine*, which she wrote between 1885 and 1888. In this *Chaldean Book of Numbers* there is contained much Wisdom which, it was claimed, was *unknown* in the West. Knowledge of it must have been gleaned from Sufis with whom she had become acquainted. She stated further that:

> Except in an Arabic work, the property of a Sufi, the writer has never met with a correct copy of these marvellous records of our past and of the future history of our globe.

There was a Babylonian connection with Blavatsky and in *Isis Unveiled*, Blavatsky explained how Sufis acquired possession of this *Chaldean Secret Doctrine*:

> During the reign of Darius, the *Chaldean* and *Brahmin Mysteries* were absorbed in the teachings of Magian initiates. They, then, according to the Roman historian Ammianus Marcellinus, cited in the text, handed down through their descendants how the Sufis, composed chiefly of Persians and Syrians, acquired their profound knowledge of astrology, medicine and the esoteric doctrine of the Ages (4).

Another seeker of Truth within living memory was George Ivanovitch Gurdjieff. He was born sometime in the 1870s in Alexandropol, in the Caucasus region of what had become Russia. He had a Greek father and an Armenian mother. The date of birth on his passport was 28 November 1877, although it is believed that he was born a bit earlier, possibly in 1872.

Gurdjieff practised as a healer in St. Petersburg, Russia from 1910 until 1917. It was there that Gurdjieff met Peter Ouspensky who, in due course, would become a disciple of Gurdjieff.

During the Russian Revolution Gurdjieff left Russia. By 1922 he had settled in Fontainebleau, France, where there would be the establishment of *The Institute for the Harmonious Development of Man*.

The passage in the writings of Gurdjieff which most specifically cites the source of his Teachings is from a book entitled *Meetings with Remarkable Men*. There we read of how the young Gurdjieff discovered a collection of letters from one monk to another in the ruins of an ancient Armenian town.

In the letters, mention was made of a Society which was referred to as the Sarmoun Brotherhood, which was reckoned to be a famous Esoteric School which, also according to Tradition, had been founded in Babylon as far back as 2500 BC. After this, Gurdjieff, as one of a group referred to as *The Seekers of Truth*, proceeded to travel through Central Asia to discover this Sarmoun Brotherhood.

In due course, and this is the conclusion of *Meetings with Remarkable Men*, the pilgrims actually arrive at the Sarmoun Monastery which was located near Chitral, in the mountains to the north of the Khyber Pass, along the present border between Pakistan and Afghanistan. Among the adepts at the monastery there were *former* Christians, Jews, Mohammedans, Buddhists, Lamaists and Shamanists but they were now all united by 'God and the Truth'.

In a book entitled *The People of the Secret* the author, Ernest Scott, relates references to a Himalayan master who belonged to the Naqshbandi Sufis. These were known as *The Masters of the Design* after their founder, Bahauddin Naqshband. Furthermore, Scott cites a traveller's account of an encounter with a centre equated with the Sarmoun Monastery. It was situated "three days north of Karachi". Scott suggested that the Sarmoun Brotherhood was a specialised sub-division of the Naqshbandi Sufis.

II

The belief that there was a *Secret Doctrine* which pertained to a Truth concerning the Origin and Destiny of the Human Race and which had been *withheld* for some reason was very much in existence during the first century AD. We know this from the New Testament.

The Apostle Paul, who is often depicted as the greatest fashioner of Christian belief, tells us that:

> Christ did not send me to baptise but to preach the Gospel, and not with eloquent wisdom lest the cross of Christ be emptied of its power (5).

Then he continues:

> Yet among the mature we do impart wisdom, although it is not the wisdom of this Age or the rulers of this Age, who are doomed to pass away. But we impart a *secret* and *hidden* wisdom of God, which God decreed *before* this Age for our glorification (6).

The Apostle Paul also tells us that the reason why he and others are incapable of revealing all is that, at this time we see *as through a glass darkly*, a passage the Apostle has borrowed directly from the writings of Plato (7).

We see, then, that there has always been the belief in a *Secret Doctrine* for the uncovering of which *Initiation* was necessary and this only for those who were considered worthy and therefore *suitable*; this had to do with the Origin and Destiny of the Human Race and *why* the Human Race exists.

It also taught that the Knowledge which we seek comes as Recollection (8) and that it does not exist in isolation for it stands in opposition to what was referred to as *The Royal Lie*. Why should this be the case?

It is here that we have to return to the Western Philosophical Tradition and to Plato whose influence upon the Western Philosophical Tradition, of which the Bible is but *a facet*, has been paramount.

When the author (John Houston) was studying these things one of the defining moments was when a passage from the historian *Flavius Josephus* presented itself, for it stated:

> Nay, Plato himself confesseth that it is not wise to publish the *true* notion concerning God amongst the ignorant multitude (9).

Elsewhere we read:

> Plato's blueprint for an ideal community has been the subject of inspiration and execration for almost 2500 years. This writing has shocked some people by its proposal of equality for women and the possession of all things in common, including wives and children. It has shocked others by its portrayal of an authoritarian, hierarchical state, with a *guardian elite*, a philosopher-king, and a *Royal Lie* to keep the masses content (10).

But what was this *Royal Lie*? Where did the Human Race encounter it? Living as we do in what was once Christendom, the Royal Lie, as we might expect, involved the proclamations of *The Cult of Jesus Christ*. It has become the opinion of the author (John Houston) that *The Royal Lie* is the Christian Gospel and the Antichrist is Jesus of Nazareth.

In centuries now gone, people were brought up under the authority of *The Cult of Jesus Christ* and, accordingly, *indoctrinated* to believe that, having been tainted with Original Sin, they would need to live their lives in the hope of experiencing salvation from their inherited, *fallen* condition. People were led to believe that they were ultimately *dependent* upon the Catholic Priesthood for the relinquishing of sins and redemption from a fallen life. If that isn't a lie, what is?

The Christian Faith as we know it now does not come from the first century AD at all, although the Christian community would obviously claim otherwise. Certainly the New Testament depicts scenes which took place, supposedly, in the Israel of the first century AD; however, the Christian Faith as we know it *now* comes from the fourth century AD and from *The Council of Nicea*, in 325 AD.

The Council of Nicea had been brought together by the Emperor Constantine to settle the terms of *The Apostles' Creed*. The final part of the

Creed which begins after "I believe in the Holy Ghost" was added later at *The Council of Constantinople* in 381 AD.

The New Testament is *not* an historical document as such. The New Testament is *mythological* rather than historical. Since the Jesus of the New Testament was actually *rejected* by the people of the first century AD, he would need to be portrayed in some other way (11); indeed it was this *Religion of Rome* which proclaimed Jesus of Nazareth as the Saviour of the world which *plunged* Europe into the Dark Ages (12).

The Jesus of the New Testament was a culturally conditioned figure, someone who was *mistaken* in his conviction that the Kingdom of God and the end of the world would come within a few years of his life, death and resurrection. This Jesus of the New Testament who was proclaimed as *The Messiah*, whose task was to establish a supernatural Kingdom on Earth and who died *voluntarily* to give his life's work its final consecration, *never existed.*

When it was obvious that the claims made by Jesus of Nazareth about his significance for us had been patently discredited *The Cult of Jesus Christ* became a Gentile phenomenon and, thereafter, this person who was born King of the Jews (13) was used as a focal point to unite Gentile Europe under Roman rule.

III

We see, then, that *The Cult of Jesus Christ* emanates from the fourth century AD, although it seeks to portray itself as originating in the first century AD in modern Israel; thus the New Testament is *not historical* as such.

It is for this reason that the New Testament and New Testament Theology is addressed to the Greek world with its first century foundation in Israel lost forever. This is something of which Martin Buber, the Jewish philosopher, seeks to remind us. He states:

> Modern Christian attempts to get back to a primal pre-Hellenistic Christianity are legion. They are also doomed.
> There never was any pre-Hellenistic Christianity. The soil on which Christianity was born had soaked up Hellenism for more than three centuries. Paul wrote his Epistles in Greek, and he

was a Hellenising Jew... a Jew, to be sure and deeply beholden to Judaism, but a Hellenistic Jew and not by any stretch of the imagination a *pre*-Hellenistic Jew. And the four Gospels were written somewhat later than were Paul's Epistles... of course, Christianity did not deny its roots in Judaism. Jesus, the Son of God, who had ascended to the heavens to dwell there with God *as God* did not simply become another Herakles, the Son of Zeus who had ascended to the heavens to dwell there with the gods, *as a god*. He did not simply become another of the legion of Greek gods and demi-gods and Sons of Zeus (14).

Plato, in time, was to be hailed as a Son of Apollo; Plato's own nephew, Speusippos, had already credited Plato with having had a miraculous birth (15).

Alexander the Great, at *The Temple of Jupiter Ammon* in Egypt, was declared to be a Son of Jupiter; accordingly he was to disavow his father, Philip of Macedon, after which, in Egypt, he was recognised as a Son of God.

Justin Martyr, in his *First Apology* which was addressed to the Emperor Hadrian wrote that "the Son of God called Jesus, even if *only a man by ordinary generation*, yet on account of his wisdom is worthy to be called Son of God... and if we affirm that he was born of a Virgin, accept this in common with what we accept of Perseus".

This mythological approach was in order to identify with an Esoteric Tradition which is as old as the Human Race; but with Rome there was to be a very real difference. The message of the New Testament was to be *literalised* for Rome was to insist that it be believed *literally*.

A process began by means of which the Romans were to *impose their Religion* on the world under their authority and, in this, the British Isles were no exception. It was by means of the Norman Invasion of 1066 that the Religion of Rome was to be *imposed* on both Great Britain and Ireland.

William the Conqueror, by means of a network of connections, was able to win approval for his invasion of England in 1066 when he acted as *Catholicism's Crusader*. Because of this he had been presented with a banner from the Pope, a banner which was at the head of his army when he led his troops into *The Battle of Hastings*, a scene which is depicted in the Bayeux Tapestry (16).

Norman and Papal ambition did not end there, however, for in 1155 authority was gained from the Pope and there was a Papal Bull *authorising the conquest of Ireland*; the Papal Bull was issued by Pope Adrian IV and was obtained by John of Salisbury.

Overlordship of the entire British Isles was the aim of the Norman Invasion and by 1157 Malcolm IV, King of Scots, was to surrender Northumberland, Cumberland and Westmorland. There was less success in the Norman attempts to subjugate Wales although there had been attacks on Gwynedd and Anglesey (17).

Fundamental to the subjection of the British Isles and the imposition of *The Religion of Rome* (which is *how* the Royal Lie was propagated), it was believed by some that the Norman Invasion sought to bring an end to certain beliefs that the British had about themselves, which figured in the Myth of Diana.

According to legend, the Goddess Diana had told the Trojan Brutus to seek out an island in the ocean which was "beyond the setting Sun" and which was also "beyond the realms of Gaul". There Brutus would be able to found a second Troy and from Brutus there would descend a line of kings who would make subject "the circle of the whole Earth" (18).

The prophecy of the Goddess Diana existed to explain the ambivalent position of Britain which, although it lies on the periphery of the Earth and "beyond the setting of the Sun" as seen from the centre, its rulers originate from the centre and are *destined* to return there to *rule*.

The native or more indigenous outlooks of the British Isles were being steadily undermined by a system which was so strong.

> The decline of Celtic influence extended to religion; until the thirteenth century Columba (Colmcille) was the unchallenged Patron Saint, his reliquary, *the Brechennach*, providing the talisman for Scottish armies in the field. But, latterly, the East coast Saints Andrew and Ninian, who deprecated the Celtic tradition, supplanted Columba; Canmore's English Queen, Margaret, had been canonised in 1250.
>
> Celtic Laws also retreated, the ancient traditions clinging to the remoter fastnesses of Galloway and the West, where Norman influence was much slower to intrude. Tanistry (19) was steadily supplanted by primogeniture. Despite the move away from the ancient Celtic past, Scottish kings continued to boast of their impressive genealogies, their descent from the fabled Irish

heroes of old. If Celticism lost its hold on the Church and on the Law, it never quite lost its grip on the imagination (20).

Native British Civilisation was to decline, so much so in fact that only vestiges were to remain. Yet the British Isles were to reaffirm their identity *as separate* from Europe and were able to gain independence from Europe; not only that but, in due course, the British were to establish the largest and most liberal Empire the world has yet seen.

The key to British self-assertion in the world was made possible by the Reformation.

> Christopher Hill, in his definitive *The English Bible and the Seventeenth Century Revolution*, says the Bible "played a large part in moulding English nationalism, in asserting the supremacy of the English language in a society which from the eleventh to the fourteenth century had been dominated by French-speaking Normans". In authorising the publication of an English version of the Bible, Henry VIII "had been mainly concerned to secure England's political independence from the Papacy". Thus it was to play a crucial part in the struggle to establish the world's first totally self-contained nation-state (21).

A situation arose, possibly on account of those Ancient Traditions relating to the Myth of Diana whereby the British felt *chosen*, a sentiment which also extended to the Americans.

> Thus the great narratives of the Old Testament have always figured strongly in Protestantism. Some historians have suggested that, lacking a history of their own, Americans were all the happier to adopt the history of the Ancient Israelites as a substitute. Before that, the early English Protestants could well have found a similar advantage. Treating the history of the Israelites as a sort of English pre-history distracted attention from that other history closer to hand, the history of England as a Catholic country of which the Puritans, if they thought about it at all, were either in denial or ashamed (22).

Now as we stand at the crossroads of Destiny for the Human Race what can we expect to see happening? The author (John Houston) believes that we will see the resurrection of the British Empire with the English-speaking nations, and others, establishing a *New World Order* which will be built upon the English language and which, in terms of the Philosophy of Religion, will go *beyond* Protestantism to the advent of *The Kingdom of God* on Earth.

The Royal Lie will have been laid to rest and in line with the True Renaissance, *The True Religion* will appear. *The Secret Doctrine* will have been made known and understood by a Humanity which is now sufficiently prepared to receive it, because this Secret Doctrine is *about* Humanity and *why* Humanity exists.

NOTES

(1) Henry S. Olcott, *Old Diary Leaves*, Volume 1, page 76.

(2) Muslim Mysticism was generally referred to as Sufism, derived from the word *Sufi*, which was someone who wore *Suf*, or undyed wool. The Sufi wore wool because of the simplicity and asceticism involved.

   The early Sufis were moved by the desire to purify the corrupt streams of Orthodox piety. Asceticism gave way to hunger for the attainment of Knowledge or Illumination. The fear of God gave way to the love of God, and the desire for union with God through *the naughting of Self*.

   Perhaps it is no surprise that Sufism had an early home in Khorasan, in Iran, where Buddhist influences had been particularly strong.

(3) H.P. Blavatsky, *The Eastern Gupta Vidya and the Kaballah*. From *The Collected Writings*, Volume 14, page 174.

(4) H.P. Blavatsky, *Isis Unveiled. The Theosophical Publishing Society*, Volume 11, page 305.

(5) *The First Epistle of Paul to the Corinthians*, Chapter 1.17.

(6) *The First Epistle of Paul to the Corinthians*, Chapter 2.7.

(7) *The First Epistle of Paul to the Corinthians*, Chapter 13.9-12.

In addition to this, from *The Phaedrus* of Plato we read:

> But not all souls do easily recall the things of the other world…
> Few only retain an adequate remembrance of them; and they,
> when they behold *here* any image of that *other world*… are rapt
> in amazement; but they are ignorant of what that rapture means,
> because they do not clearly perceive… they are seen as through a
> glass dimly; and there are few who, going to the images, behold
> in them the realities, and these only with difficulty.

(8) Furthermore, from *The Meno* of Plato we read:

> and it is no wonder that she should be able to call to remembrance
> all that she ever knew about Virtue, and about everything; for as
> all Nature is akin, and the soul has learned all things, there is no
> difficulty in her eliciting or as men say *learning*, out of a single
> recollection of the rest, if a man is strenuous and does not faint,
> for *all* enquiry and *all* learning are but recollection.

(9) *The Complete Works of Flavius Josephus*. Translated by William Whiston,
Professor of Mathematics at the University of Cambridge. Published by
The London Printing and Publishing Company Limited. From the edition
held at *The Mitchell Library* in Glasgow, Scotland. From the chapter,
Flavius Josephus against Apion, Book II, page 560.

(10) Mortimer J. Adler and Peter Wolff. *The Development of Political Theory
and Government*. Book 2 in the series, *The Great Ideas Program*. Published
by *The Encyclopaedia Britannica, Inc.* in Chicago in 1959, page 1.
     On page 13 of the above-mentioned book we read:

> Plato, therefore, means a union of the philosopher's and the
> statesman's virtues that must be sufficiently deep so that all
> political acts of the philosopher-king are wise, and so that all
> his political thought is directed towards political ends. Here,
> of course, we must ask whether such a union is possible. Not
> only must we question the practical possibility of ever finding a
> philosopher king for Plato would be quick enough to agree that
> such a possibility is very slight.

(11) The *rejection* of Jesus of Nazareth by the people of the first century AD was for several reasons.

The claims that Jesus of Nazareth made about his return to Earth from Heaven to establish his Kingdom with a corresponding end of the world as we know it did *not* happen.

On another level the Jews would have rejected Jesus of Nazareth because they believed that this Jesus had undermined the grace of God, indeed Jesus held beliefs which were at variance with *The Law of Moses*.

Fundamental to *The Law of Moses* was the belief that anyone who seeks sincerely to return to God may do so and, *if* their desire is sincere, they will be *freely* forgiven. The Christian Gospel *denies* this; indeed the proclamation relating to the *atoning death* of Christ as the pre-requisite for salvation *presupposes* that God *cannot* freely forgive.

The fact that, in the New Testament, the Jews are seen to reject Jesus of Nazareth is fertile ground for anti-Semitism; such is the opinion of the author (John Houston). Thereafter, the formulators of the New Testament and of New Testament Theology utilised the figure of the Gnostic Redeemer as *one* of the ways of portraying Jesus.

As has been dealt with in *The Sacred Ibis Speaks* and from the essay *Christ as Hermes; the Great Magician,* the problems facing the Christian apologists in relation to *how* they would portray Jesus to the Gentiles was not satisfactorily resolved until they used the figure of Socrates as a model. As was common knowledge at the time, Socrates was viewed as the wisest man in the Ancient World.

(12) Bertrand Russell, *The History of Western Philosophy.* With an Introduction by A.C. Grayling. Published in London by *The Folio Society* in 2004. From the seventh chapter entitled, *Athens in Relation to Culture.* See page 60.

Bertrand Russell states:

In spite of political collapse, the prestige of Athens survived and throughout almost a millennium philosophy was centred there. Alexandria eclipsed Athens in Mathematics and Science, but Plato and Aristotle made Athens philosophically supreme. The Academy, where Plato had taught, survived all other Schools and persisted as an island of Paganism, for two centuries after the conversion of the Roman Empire to Christianity. At last, in 529 AD, it was closed by Justinian because of his religious bigotry, and the Dark Ages descended upon Europe.

(13) *The Gospel according to Matthew*, Chapter 2.2.

(14) Martin Buber, *I and Thou*. Translated from the German by Walter Kaufmann. Published by T&T Clark, Edinburgh in 1970. See page 34.

(15) John Burnet, *Greek Philosophy*. Published by *The MacMillan Press*, 1981 edition. Page 167.

(16) M.T. Clanchy, *England and Its Rulers 1066–1272*. A Fontana Original. *The Fontana History of England Series*. Published by Fontana Paperbacks in 1983. From the fourth chapter, *Church Reform*. See page 90f.

(17) As (16) above. From Chapter Five, *The Struggles for the Kingdom*, page 129.

(18) As (16) above. From the chapter, *England's Place in Medieval Europe*, page 26.

(19) John Sadler, *Bannockburn. Battle for Liberty*. Published by *Pen & Sword Military* in 2008.

   Pen & Sword Military is an imprint of Pen & Sword Books Limited, 47 Church Street, Barnsley, South Yorkshire, S70 2AS.

   Tanistry was a Celtic system for inheritance whereby the successful candidate, or *Tanist*, was elected from a particular class or category of eligible claimants. This may sound democratic but was the stuff of mayhem as claimants sought to level the odds by eliminating rivals.

(20) As (19) above. See page 6.

(21) Clifford Longley, *Chosen People*. The big idea that shapes England and America. Published by Hodder & Stoughton in 2002. See page 65.

(22) As (21) above. See page 33.

3: Plethon & Giovanni

I

In 1438 there had been a Church Council in Ferrera but it had all come to nothing. The following year there was another one and this time it was held in Florence.

Quite naturally, the Pope had favoured the move to Florence since Florence had been the Pope's principal residence since his expulsion from Rome in 1434.

Florence was also home to a man by the name of Cosimo de' Medici, a very important man in many ways. By 1434, Cosimo de' Medici had *not only* inherited the role of Papal banker but was recognised as the most powerful citizen in Florence in his own right. Cosimo de' Medici was able to guarantee that Florence would be able to meet the costs of *The Council*.

While at *The Council of Florence* in 1439, Cosimo de' Medici on several occasions had listened intently to a Greek philosopher known as George Gemistos Plethon. Cosimo had been powerfully moved. Plethon had spoken like a *second Plato*, of Platonism and how what was really, truly required was a *School of Philosophy* along Platonic lines. There and then Plethon had put into the mind of Cosimo de' Medici the desire to found such a School of Philosophy "when the opportunity presented itself".

These were no ordinary men and this was no ordinary time. Much would go on behind the scenes involving *esoteric philosophy*, the consideration of one *Hermes Trismegistus*, whom esotericists referred to as *The Messenger of the gods*. A movement would be brought to life whose aim was to *replace* Jesus Christ and the prophet Muhammed with Hermes Trismegistus. This was fundamental to the intention to accomplish the *Hermetic Reformation* of Christianity and Islam; but there was more.

> Ames-Lewis suggested that Plethon's chief contribution to the education of members of the Medici circle attending the Council was not primarily, as is usually assumed, to give them a new knowledge of Platonism, but to introduce to them the text of Strabo's work on astronomy. This subject, together with the related cult of astrology, fascinated many Florentines, and especially the members of the Medici family (1).

The Florence of the day had a fascination for *the unknown* and was thrilled by the exotic. All sorts of things were happening and it would appear that Cosimo de' Medici was at the hub of it, like a great life-enlarging mentor to the people of his city. We know that Cosimo de' Medici had a great interest in Cartography as well as the writings of the Ancient Philosophers (2).

Years later, in 1463, Cosimo de' Medici felt able to put his plans for the appearance of a School of Philosophy along Platonic lines into action. For his purpose, he had chosen the young Marsilio Ficino, son of the physician Dietifeci, and had supervised his education.

In due course, Cosimo de' Medici thought that the time had come for the young Marsilio Ficino to be supplied with manuscripts pertaining to Plato and Plotinus. In 1463 Cosimo de' Medici *commissioned* Marsilio Ficino to translate writings *relating to Hermes Trismegistus*. This is not to be wondered at for when Cosimo was having Marsilio Ficino educated it was *to this end* that Ficino's education had tended.

Later in his life, in 1490 in fact, Marsilio Ficino recalled those circumstances to Lorenzo de' Medici.

> But later, in 1463, he (Cosimo) charged me with translating first Mercury Trismegistus and then Plato (3).

It may seem strange that Cosimo should have asked the young Ficino to translate those writings pertaining to Hermes or Mercury Trismegistus *before* attempting Plato; at the time the West was still awaiting a complete translation of the latter.

Cosimo de'Medici must also have had a great desire to read those Hermetic Texts and acquaint himself fully with the Hermetic Tradition. As soon as the Texts arrived in Florence they were sent immediately for translation. They were brought from Macedonia by a monk named Leonardo da Pistoia (4). The manuscripts contained what we now recognise as the first fifteen Treatises of *The Corpus Hermeticum* (5).

Another indication of the excitement with which the Hermetic Texts were received in Florentine circles is the fact that Ficino's Latin version was immediately rendered into the vernacular by his fellow philosopher, Tommaso Benci, in September 1463.

The reason for the high expectation aroused by the arrival of the translation of *The Corpus Hermeticum* is explained by Ficino himself. Based on the Testimonies of men such as Cicero, or Lactantius or by Saint Augustine it was to be expected that there would be *a great antiquity* to Hermes Trismegistus.

What was falling into place of its own accord, indeed, was the realisation that the Hermes of the Greeks, or the Mercury of the Romans or Thoth of the ibis beak, the Egyptian Hermes and the *mythical* Inventor of Writing were all one and the same person. Worshipped as a god in Egypt, Mercury had acquired the title *Trismegistus* or 'thrice-greatest' because he was at the same time, *philosophus maximus, sacerdos maximus and rex maximus* (6).

As far as the *historicity* of Hermes Trismegistus is concerned and the *ancientness* of the Hermetic Tradition encapsulated in *The Corpus Hermeticum*, neither Ficino nor the Humanists of the Renaissance entertained a doubt, for much had been vouched for by the great Authorities of Antiquity and of *early* Christianity.

Hymns to Hermes and other gods or goddesses were sung as preludes or *prooimia* to recitations of stories from the great *Epics*. They were sung at Festivals associated with contests such as the Games which followed the Festival at Delphi in honour of the Snake Goddess, or the Games in Nemea in honour of the Mountain God.

From the time of the Games in the fifth century BC until an edition from Demetrios Chalcondyles in Florence in 1488, the hymns were virtually ignored. One such referred to the beautiful Maia, the mother of Hermes. She had shunned the company of the gods, preferring to live alone in a cave in the side of Mount Kyllene.

> Sing to Me, Muse, of Hermes Son of Zeus and Maia.
> Guardian of Kyllene and Arkadia with its sheep
> The Messenger of the gods
> The Luck-bringer whom Maia mothered.
> Born at dawn he was playing the lyre that afternoon
> In the evening he misappropriated cattle belonging to Apollo.

Citations from Lactantius concerning the Teachings attributed to Hermes Trismegistus state that there was *an apparent affinity* between the philosophy of Hermes and of Plato, especially in the work known as *The Timaeus*. He would go further, stating that Hermes had been *a contemporary* of the Biblical Moses and that he had surpassed *all* the philosophers of Antiquity. He included Hermes "among the Sybils and the Prophets", indeed "a Pagan Prophet of the Christian Revelation".

Tertullian recognised Hermes as "The Teacher of all Philosophers". In *The Sibylline Oracles*, Hermes is mentioned twice as *an Egyptian god*. Diodorus believed that it had been Hermes who had introduced religious worship to the Egyptians; furthermore, he was also the Inventor of Alphabets, Articulate Speech, Eloquence and Music.

Cicero had been told that Hermes had provided Law and instruction in the Sciences for the benefit of *all* Humanity. Plato, himself, is reputed to have stated that Hermes had provided instruction in Grammar, Arithmetic, Geometry, Astronomy and Astrology.

Then there is Medicine, which Asclepius is said to have inherited from Hermes, not to mention Alchemy, which for the period of 1500 years was sole claimant to the title, *Hermetic Art*.

As it happens all of this was of *secondary* importance for Marsilio Ficino, in comparison to the contribution Hermes Trismegistus had made with his Philosophical-Theological Writings, and to the establishment of a *Prisca Theologia*, an Ancient Religion which was, or so it seemed, so much in accordance with the Bible.

The great significance of *The Corpus Hermeticum* provided by the young Marsilio Ficino was that the Latin West was, for the first time, confronted with a complete set of Teachings of which only a fragment, *The Book of Asclepius*, had been available in the West, in Latin. It is hardly surprising that, of all of

Ficino's works, it was *The Pimander* which was the most assiduously copied, with the printed copies having closely followed each other.

The shockwave which ensued after the dissemination of the Hermetic Literature, or *The Corpus Hermeticum*, into Western culture can only be described as *epochal*. Western Christianity suddenly found itself face to face with a second *Divine Revelation* which was even clearer than the Bible.

For many there was the satisfaction that the West had received a welcome confirmation of the truth of the Christian Revelation; other, more profound, minds found in *The Corpus Hermeticum* fertile soil for far-reaching philosophical and theological speculations which could not be reconciled with Christian Orthodoxy (7).

The destruction of the Hermetic Tradition and Culture which had prevailed in the North African provinces of the Roman Empire had been unfortunate. Hermetism had been unrelentingly suppressed by the victorious *Cult of Jesus Christ* and hunted to extinction. It had all gone, or so it seemed, despite the posthumous Christianisation of Hermes Trismegistus and his annexation by Christian Apologists. Only a few pitiful crumbs remained and it was to Marsilio Ficino's merit that such hidden treasure was brought to light after a thousand years.

Ficino was to describe Hermes as *Primus Auctor Theologiae*, the first Founder of Theology. He was to place Hermes at the head of a *Catena* of Ancient Theologians, *the Prisci Theologi*, whose Teachings were essentially in agreement. There was Hermes, then there was Orpheus, Aglaophemus, Pythagoras, Philolaus and then Plato.

This *Catena* of *Prisci Theologi* given by Ficino in his *Argumentum* was introduced by Proclus in *The Theology of Plato*. Ficino made a novel contribution by placing Hermes, *not* mentioned by Proclus who lists only *Greek* Theologians, at the *beginning* of the series. The precedence given to the translation of Hermes over that of Plato is thus explained by the *great antiquity* of Hermes, the *Egyptian* Sage, whose Revelation would now be passed on to future generations.

In his *Argumentum*, Ficino emphasises the *prophetic* character of the theological works of Hermes Trismegistus. In terms of Doctrine, two works are mentioned: the first of these is entitled *The Asclepius* and the second is entitled *The Pimander*.

Yet Ficino was to discover that *The Asclepius* and *The Pimander* were not the complete *Corpus Hermeticum*. There were other Treatises, that is, numbers sixteen to eighteen (XVI to XVIII) which had escaped Ficino's notice simply because they were lacking from the Codex which he received (8).

The Asclepius was translated by Apuleius and *The Pimander* by Marsilio Ficino; Treaties XVI to XVIII were to be translated by Ludovico Lazzarelli and they were to become known as *The Definitiones Asclepii* (9).

II

By this time, however, *George Gemistos Plethon* was dead and buried. But who was he? What was he seeking to achieve? What kind of vision did he follow?

Plethon was probably the first competent interpreter of Plato and Aristotle to address a Latin audience *in Greek* for over a thousand years. At the time of his arrival in Florence in 1439 the process of translating Plato into Latin was in its early stages. On the other hand, the translation of Aristotle was *complete*.

It was not until 1423 that the complete *Corpus* of Plato's surviving writings was available in the West, even in the original Greek. The philosophical study of Plato, as distinct from the literary task of translation, had scarcely begun; but it began *in earnest* with the arrival of Plethon.

When Marsilio Ficino came into contact with the Platonism of George Gemistos Plethon two incontrovertible points can be deduced from the outcome. It seems Ficino sought to link his own Platonic career with that of Plethon (10).

From the time that Marsilio Ficino had started to learn Greek, which was in 1456, he devoted all his energies to the translation of those Authors whom Plethon had indicated (11); because of this, we are able to reconstruct the succession of translations made from Greek by Marsilio Ficino. It appears to indicate a significant parallel with the Teachings of Plethon, especially with regard to the *Sapiental Catena* of the Ancient Theologians.

Plethon had long considered Zoroaster and his disciples to be the first Guardians of Truth, locating their Teachings to a time much earlier than either Moses or Hermes Trismegistus; indeed of these two Plethon makes *no* mention. Plethon claimed that Pythagoras, *the Ionian*, had introduced the Teachings of Zoroaster to the Greeks, and from them to Plato.

Orpheus is cited as the Guardian of Hellenic (Greek) Theology, which was cultivated in remote times by *The Kouretes*, mystical priests of Zeus who had lived on the isle of Crete. For Plethon they were the earliest of the Greek Sages and their Doctrines were in accordance with Zoroaster.

Plethon regarded the Egyptian Traditions such as those of Diodorus Siculus, or of Eusebius of Caesarea or of Diogenes Laertius, as part of Traditions which were *the daughter* of Zoroastrianism.

In Ficino's writings the *Catena* of *Prisci Theologi*, who are always six in number, assume various configurations. Only in *The Proemium* to *The Pimander* does Philolaus appear, between Pythagoras and Plato, and there is *no* Zoroaster. The order is Mercury Trismegistus, Orpheus, Aglaophemus, Pythagoras, Philolaus and then Plato.

In *The Commentarium in Philebum* of 1469, in *De Christiana Religione* and in *The Theologia Platonica* (The Theology of Plato), Zoroaster appears at the head of the list and there is *no* Philolaus. In *The Theologia Platonica*, there is a clear explanation of the order of succession.

> In these matters concerning Theology, at one time six supreme Theologians were in agreement, of whom the first is said to have been Zoroaster, the leader of the Magi; the second was Mercury Trismegistus, the Prince of Egyptian priests. Orpheus succeeded Mercury, Aglaophemus was then initiated into *The Mysteries* of Orpheus, Pythagoras succeeded Aglaophemus in Theology, and Pythagoras was succeeded by Plato who, in his writings understood, increased and illustrated all their Wisdom.

It has been stated that George Gemistos Plethon had the intention of starting a *New Religion*. Some people thought this. Demetrios Raoul Kabakes was an enthusiastic admirer of Gemistos Plethon.

> There is much evidence of his devotion to Gemistos. He recorded a conversation with Bessarion, after his master's death, in which Bessarion told him that there was no wiser man in Greece since Plotinus.
>
> Under Gemistos' influence, he admired Julian the Apostate and shared his passionate love of the Sun. A curious note survives, in Kabakes' handwriting, on a manuscript of Julian's *Address to*

King Helios. Kabakes admitted that he was a Sun-worshipper and stated that Gemistos was also (12).

One Gregorios stated when informed of the death of Plethon:

> Gone is the man of much experience in secret and divine matters, the leader of initiates in high and heavenly doctrines, the amplest and godliest intellect, the divine leader in high philosophy, the man who enquired scientifically into the whole of Divine Wisdom and the whole of Human Wisdom, who through natural skill and memory and greatness of mind gathered more than a natural share of Wisdom (13).

A great Testimony came from Cardinal Bessarion, who had once been a pupil of Gemistos Plethon. He had lived in Italy since 1441 and was so highly regarded in Rome that twice, in 1455 and in 1471, he was a serious candidate for the Papacy. For him, *Plato* had come down to Earth and *assumed* the frame and life of Gemistos Plethon:

> I have learned that our common father and master has shed the earthly element and departed to Heaven, to the place of purity, joining the mystical chorus of Iacchus with Olympian gods. I, too, rejoice to have studied with such a man, the wisest that Greece has produced since Plato... (14).

Concerning George Gemistos Plethon, what else was said about him? One George Trapezuntius was always a very hostile witness.
Trapezuntius stated:

> It was known that Gemistos was so much a Platonist... I myself heard him at Florence, for he came to the Council with the Greeks, asserting that the whole world would in a few years adopt one and the same religion, with one mind, one intelligence, one teaching.
>
> And when I asked: Christ's or Muhammed's? He replied: Neither, but one *not* differing from Paganism.
> This answer shocked Trapezuntius, who continued,

I heard, too, from a number of Greeks who escaped here from the Peloponnese that he openly said, about three years before his death, that not many years after his death both Muhammed and Christ would be forgotten and the real truth would shine through all the shores of the world (15).

What could Plethon have meant by this? We shall turn to this in due course.

III

Because of these translations, Marsilio Ficino became the spiritual focus of *The Platonic Academy* of Florence. As the physician and philosopher, Theodor Zwinger, some hundred years later wrote in the *preface* to the *Opera* of Ficino's pupil, Francesco da Diacceto:

> It was this Academy, the influence of which has allowed us to be able to philosophise freely and elegantly.
>
> How much our *Republica Literaria* owes to the Florentine Academy can be witnessed by the fact that at the time when the darkest barbarism had pervaded all scholarship and where, subsequently, the Renaissance of the Greek and Latin languages began, the Florentine Academy was the first to have introduced the study of a purer philosophy on the basis of Platonic and Hermetic sources.

Plethon had arrived on the scene hoping to elevate the status of Plato and intent on putting those writings pertaining to Zoroaster into context, as a Philosophical Tradition whose roots were from a time *earlier* than either Moses or Hermes, who were generally considered to be *contemporaries*. It is for this reason that:

> *Hermes Mercurius Trismegistus contemporaneus Moysi* is chiselled in marble on the famous floor decorations of 1488 in the Cathedral of Siena.

This Moses and Hermes Trismegistus were *both* to be identified with the Egyptian god, Thoth of the ibis beak; at any rate Hermes did not need to be Egyptianised for, as we read in *The Suda Lexicon*, Hermes was *Egyptian* by race.

We can thus readily understand that, at the time of the Florentine Renaissance, this re-discovered Hermes Trismegistus was depicted as an Egyptian sage of impeccable religious conduct and profoundly intellectual views. He had travelled extensively proclaiming the Doctrine of the One True God, the Demiurge and Father of all, until he returned to Egypt where he compiled a great number of books concerning Mystical Philosophy and Theology.

This One True God to whom Hermes Trismegistus referred was virtually the same as the planet Earth. This was noted in various places, that Hermes held that the world was co-substantial with God, to be a *second* God, or God's Son. George Gemistos Plethon would have known this, indeed he would have rejoiced in this because *such was the outlook of Zoroaster*.

> When Zoroaster and Hermes Trismegistus claim that the world
> is a great God, I answer that this great God is Christ alone
> because he is the Almighty Lord of the world (16).

What of this New Religion which, as Plethon claimed, would shine throughout the world? It would appear that something very unusual, indeed *fantastic*, had taken place in the period not long after 1480. It involves Ludovico Lazzarelli, an enthusiastic admirer of Ficino, and the Hermetic Treatises XVI to XVIII which he had translated into Latin (17).

One day, Ludovico Lazzarelli was leafing through the codices of holy men, as was his custom, when suddenly and quite unexpectedly, he came across a small Greek book entitled *The Definitiones Asclepii*.

It was at once clear to him that he had stumbled upon a cup filled with sweet nectar, which had issued from the Divine and magnificent *Krater*, or Vessel, of Hermes Trismegistus. Lazzarelli was struck by the sublimity, the brevity and the mystical manner of this representation of Divine Wisdom. He then set about its translation.

We know that this Ludovico Lazzarelli had been a Humanist. Something had indeed happened for he was to be *converted*, so to speak. He was to become *a disciple* of the prophet, one known as Giovanni Mercurio da Correggio (18).

Lazzarelli dedicated his translation of *The Definitiones Asclepii* to his mentor and master, Giovanni da Correggio, who had made his entrance in Rome in 1484 *as the born-again Mercurius*, thereby causing an enormous sensation. The translation was probably completed sometime between 1484 and 1492 (19).

In imitation of his master Giovanni Mercurio, Lazzarelli provided himself with the epithet *Enoch,* who was reputed to have been *the first revelation* of Hermes among the Arabs. Now, in 1484, there was *another manifestation* of Hermes although not restricted to the Arabs, for it was addressed to the entire Human Race.

In effect, there was in 1484, *the miraculous appearance of a Divine Prophet* who called for the *Hermetic Reformation* of Christianity and Islam, involving the intention of *replacing* both Jesus Christ and the Prophet Muhammed with Hermes Trismegistus.

Plethon therefore considered Enoch, as a manifestation of Hermes Trismegistus, to be *synonymous* with the prophet Muhammed (20); and here we may touch upon rather vague, indeed exceptionally obscure tales of the one known as *Johann Hoffmann,* which refer to his unrivalled music ability, as the Germans noted.

Johann Hoffmann was enshrouded in mystery even then; very few people knew him and the location of his home was kept secret. His few close associates referred to him as Giovanni.

In referring to this *manifestation* of Hermes, Lazzarelli employs antiquated Biblical-style language. He would speak of Giovanni Mercurio da Correggio, whose appearance was that of *an Angel of Divine Wisdom*, for the prophet Giovanni da Correggio was recognised as *the Reincarnation of Pimander*, one who used magical and kabbalistic rituals as part of his *performances*.

At any rate, Lazzarelli quotes as though from the New Testament:

This is my Son, *Pimander,* whom I have chosen (21).

This was further enriched with borrowings from *The Tabula Smaragdina*, from the supplements to the book *Raziel*, from *The Almadel* of Solomon and from *The Liber Septem Planetarum* of Hermes.

With this *Krater* of Hermes, Lazzarelli attempted to prove the *absolute equality* of the Biblical Revelation and the Hermetic Wisdom which was of *Egyptian* origin.

In the first sentences of a *fictitious* dialogue between Lazzarelli and King Ferdinand of Aragon, Lazzarelli writes that:

> What Pimander was in the mind of Hermes, this Christ is in me (22).
>
> And, at the end of the dialogue he repeats, thus I will praise Christ under the name of Pimander, which was interpreted by Hermes *as Mind* as well as *Word of Divine Omnipotence* (23).

Lazzarelli's outlook was simple indeed; without difficulty, he saw himself as a Christian and as a Hermetist at the same time (24). Lazzarelli, the translator, had dedicated his version of the last books of *The Corpus Hermeticum* to his master, Giovanni Mercurio. He signed his name as Ludovicus *Enoch* Lazzarellus who used to be a mere poet, but now he greets the master as *Regenerate Son of True Wisdom*.

NOTES

(1) Dale Kent, *Cosimo de' Medici and the Florentine Renaissance*. Published by Yale University Press, New Haven and London in 2000, page 155.

(2) Dale Kent, *Cosimo de' Medici and the Florentine Renaissance*. Published by Yale University Press, New Haven and London in 2000.

According to Lippincott in *Art of Cartography*, this was one of the few areas of scientific endeavour in which the Florentines were pre-eminent. A thirteenth century illuminated copy of Ptolemy's *Geographia* was left by Manuel Chrysoloras at his death in 1415 to Palla Strozzi, and became the source of all such maps in Italy.

Ptolemy's *Geographia* was translated into Latin by Iacobo d'Angelo in the first decades of the fifteenth century. The maps were copied by Francesco di Lappacino and Domenico di Lionardo Buoninsegni.

Gregorio Dati's account of the assets of his native city, extracted from his *History of Florence*, sometimes appears in compilations along with his more widely circulated popularisation, often beautifully illustrated, of classical geographical studies. Dati's *Globe* (sometimes *Sfera* or *Mappomondo*) described the three parts of the known world; Europe, Asia and Africa.

Ptolemy's *Geographia* was available in Florence by 1395. It was translated into Latin under the title *Cosmographia* in 1410. Piero de' Medici owned a set of Ptolemaic charts; in relation to the Medici interest in Astrology, Ames-Lewis also noted the Astrological Designs on the carpet of the San Marco altarpiece and the ceiling of Piero's *tempiello* in San Miniato al Monte.

(3)　*Marsilio Ficino and the Return of Hermes Trismegistus.* Published jointly by *The Biblioteca Medicea Laurenziana* in Florence and *The Bibliotheca Philosophica Hermetica* in Amsterdam in 1999, page 27.

In a famous passage in *The Proemium* to his *Commentaria in Plotinum* of 1490, Marsilio Ficino gives Lorenzo de' Medici a brief account of his own career as a translator and exegete of the Ancient Philosophers, which began with his version of *The Corpus Hermeticum*.

Ficino's translation of *The Corpus Hermeticum* into Latin was completed in April 1463.

Marsilio Ficino's sixteenth century biographer, Giovanni Corsi, stated that Cosimo de' Medici had presented the young Ficino with a villa at Careggi as a reward for his translation of *The Corpus Hermeticum*. This date is confirmed from the act recording the donation of a villa, dated 18 April 1463; this was the month and year that the translation of Hermes was completed.

(4)　This monk was also known as Leonardo Macedone.

The Greek manuscripts of *The Corpus Hermeticum* which have survived to this day all appear to go back to a copy belonging to Michael Psellus of the eleventh century. This copy of Psellus is no longer extant and there is always the possibility that it was, itself, copied from a much older prototype.

(5)　For Ficino, the complete *Corpus Hermeticum* is a single dialogue. *Pimander* has the first place; *Trismegistus* has the second place; *Asclepius* has the third place, then there is *Tat*.

In the first Treatise, *Pimander Mens Divinae Potentiae* teaches Hermes Trismegistus; in the second Treatise Hermes instructs *Asclepius*; then there is an Oration entitled *Sermo Sacer*.

After this Hermes instructs Tat; indeed Asclepius and Tat alternate as disciples of Hermes.

All Trismegistus' Doctrine is derived from the master *Pimander*, the Mind, the one who is the fount of *all* Hermetic Revelation.

The first part of *The Corpus Hermeticum* to be translated into Latin was known as *The Asclepius*; this was the work of *Apuleius*. The second part to be translated was *De Potestate et Sapientiae Dei*, also known as *The Pimander*; this was the work of Marsilio Ficino.

There were three other Treatises, omitted from the Codex used by Marsilio Ficino; these were known as *The Definitiones Asclepii*. They were to be translated by Ludovico Lazzarelli.

(6)   *The Gnostic Gospels*, edited by Marvin Meyer. Incorporating, *The Sacred Writings of the Nag Hammadi Library, The Berlin Gnostic Codex and Codex Tchacos*. Published by *The Folio Society*, London, in 2008. From *Hermetic Religion*. See page 689.

As soon as the Greeks became acquainted with Egypt, they identified the Egyptian god Thoth, the inventor of the hieroglyphs, with Hermes, the most learned of their own Deities. In Egyptian Traditions, Thoth was called "great, great and very great", as a superlative expression. Initially, this phrase was literally translated into Greek as *megas, megas, megistos*, and eventually this expression was abridged as *Trismegas*, 'thrice great', or *Trismegistos*, 'thrice greatest'. Since Greek speakers did not understand the meaning of the Egyptian superlative, they reinterpreted it in different ways.

Some Greek thinkers fancied Trismegistus as the third offspring of a lineage of Ancient Sages. As the son of Hermes-Agathodemon, he was thought to have translated into Greek and handed over to his son Hermes-Tat the hieroglyphic writings carved on steles before the Flood by their Ancestor Hermes-Thoth.

Other Greeks said that the figure was called Trismegistus because he had discovered that the Supreme God consists in a three-fold great power (mostly likely the Unbegotten, the Self-Begotten and the Begotten One).

Still other Greeks explained that Hermes had come to this world at three different times, before and after the Flood. During his third advent he 'recognised himself', and thus merited the epithet *Trismegistus*.

(7)   As a classic example we may cite Giordano Bruno, who referred to the Divine Magic of the Egyptians as a Religion, indeed a good Religion which went into decline when *The Cult of Jesus Christ* commenced what would be its eventual destruction.

The dialogue *Theophrastus* by Aeneas of Gaza which was translated by Marsilio Ficino contains information on the Ancient Religion of the Egyptians and their belief in *the transmigration of the soul*; there was also information on a 'rival' *Prisca Theologia*, concerning prophecy from the Chaldeans and from Zoroastrians concerning the resurrection of the dead.

The Chaldeans had attracted the attention of the Greeks for many centuries because of their skill in Prophecy which was recognised as far back as the fifth century BC. Plethon associated them with Zoroaster and the Persian Magi. Ficino followed Plethon in doing so.

Proclus stated that he would be content to see all literature destroyed except *The Timaeus* of Plato and *The Chaldean Oracles*.

(8)   The Codex which Marsilio Ficino had received was known as *The Codex Lauriantius*, containing only Treatises 1 to 15, or numbers I to XV.

(9)   Please refer to note (5), above.

(10) C.M. Woodhouse, *George Gemistos Plethon. The Last of the Hellenes.* Published as a special edition for Sandpiper Books Ltd., in 2000. See page 187.

(11) We should not forget the fact that Ficino knew of Plethon only at second hand, through Cosimo de' Medici. Marsilio Ficino referred to Plethon as "Plethonem quasi alterum Platonem".

(12) C.M. Woodhouse, *George Gemistos Plethon. The Last of the Hellenes.* Published as a special edition for Sandpiper Books Ltd., in 2000. See page 34.

(13) As (12) above. See page 9.

(14) As (12), above. See page 13.

(15) As (12), above. See page 168.

(16) *Marsilio Ficino and the Return of Hermes Trismegistus*. Published jointly by *The Biblioteca Medicea Laurenziana* in Florence and *The Bibliotheca Philosophica Hermetica* in Amsterdam in 1999. See page 286.

   Refer also to John Burnet, *Greek Philosophy*. Published by *The MacMillan Press Limited*, London in 1981. See page 27f.

(17) *Marsilio Ficino and the Return of Hermes Trismegistus*. Published jointly by *The Biblioteca Medicea Laurenziana* in Florence and *The Bibliotheca Philosophica Hermetica* in Amsterdam in 1999. See page 61.

   Wouter J. Hanergraaff & Ruud M. Bouthoom, *Ludovico Lazzarelli; The Hermetic Writings and Related Documents*. Published by *The Arizona Center for Medieval and Renaissance Studies* in Tempe, Arizona in 2005.

It is possible that Lazzarelli was born on 4 February 1447. It is claimed, however, by others such as Kristeller, Garin and Roellenbleck that he was born in 1450. These men have based their assumption on information from Lancillotti's biography of 1765.

To all appearances, Arianna was his first and only love. Lazzarelli never seems to have married, nor do we have any evidence of any other amorous involvement. In his later years he seems to have pursued what could be described as 'better things', a spiritual ideal of chastity and the transcendence of the bodily passions.

The year 1468 must indeed be seen as the one in which Lazzarelli reached maturity as a poet. This is also demonstrated by his *Hymn to Prometheus*, written at this time and dedicated to the Venetian Ambassador, Francesco Giustiniani. His *Hymn* combines the characteristic Humanist concern with 'the excellence of Man' (which was to culminate, obviously, in Pico della Mirandola's *Oratio de Hominis Dignitate*) with the popular contemporary topic of *The Myth of Prometheus*.

(18) Wouter J. Hanegraaff & Ruud M. Bouthoom, *Ludovico Lazzarelli; The Hermetic Writings and Related Documents*. Published by *The Arizona Center For Medieval and Renaissance Studies* in Tempe, Arizona in 2005.

The Prophet; Giovanni Mercurio da Correggio

Our most detailed source of information about Correggio is *The Epistola Enoch* which describes his appearances in Rome in 1481 and 1484. The *Enoch* who introduces himself as its author is certainly a pseudonym adopted by Lazzarelli. In addition, we have a smattering of smaller documents and scraps of evidence, including a description of Correggio's later appearance in Lyons written by Johannes Trithemius.

The first problem confronting us in these sources concerns the question of Correggio's year of birth, which cannot be established with certainty. According to *The Epistola Enoch*, when Correggio appeared in Rome in 1484 "he looked about thirty-three years old".

We might therefore be tempted to conclude that he was born in or around 1451. More importantly, the similarity of Jesus' age of thirty-three is unlikely to be a coincidence. We will see that Correggio's entrance into Rome on Palm Sunday 1484, as described in *The Epistola Enoch*, was closely modelled on the Biblical story of Jesus' entrance into Jerusalem.

Likewise, Lazzarelli's description of Correggio's physical appearance deliberately tries to suggest a close similarity with the popular image of Jesus. Mentioning an age of "about thirty-three" may therefore have been inspired simply by Lazzarelli's wish to emphasise the parallels, *unless* it was Correggio himself who, believing that he was Christ reincarnate, decided it would be appropriate to wait for his thirty-third year to make his appearance in Rome on Palm Sunday.

He may have been born in or around 1451; the available evidence indicates that he came from a well-known, old and powerful family belonging to the higher nobility, had a house in Bologna at least well into the 1490s and suffered no serious financial problems.

Most likely, he was a bastard son of Antonio da Correggio, one of the five sons of Gherardo da Correggio. Antonio's two marriages had failed to produce an heir which is why it is assumed that Giovanni was illegitimate.

Apart from this, nothing is to be found or inferred about his early life and how he turned into the strange prophet who made his first documented appearance in Rome on 12 November 1481.

The first Roman appearance in 1481 is described in *The Epistola Enoch*; in Rome the Cardinals were gathering for a *Consistory Meeting*, an event of considerable importance for it would have had to do with *Ecclesiastical Law*.

The Second Roman appearance took place on the 11 April 1484. There is mention of this in *The Epistola Enoch* and there is also confirmation of this from one Giuliano Fantaguzzi from the town of Casena. It appears that Correggio actually claimed to be the true Messiah.

The Epistola Enoch tells us that 1484 was a year already filled with popular hopes and expectations of a spiritual *renovatio*, due to the occurrence of a great conjunction between the planets Saturn and Jupiter and Palm Sunday was the high point of the year.

It is alleged that Giovanni da Correggio carried a large text stating "this is my Servant Pimander, whom I have chosen. This Pimander is my supreme and waxing child in whom I am well pleased."

He was later to proclaim, "I, Giovanni Mercurio of Correggio, the Angel of Wisdom Pimander, in the highest and greatest ecstacy of the spirit of Christ Jesus evangelize loudly unto all this water of the Kingdom for the few."

(19) As (17), above. See page 128.

(20) We are informed of Enoch in *The Book of Genesis*, Chapter 5. He is reputed to have lived for 365 years after which he was *translated*, that is, he was directly taken up to Heaven for he had pleased God. Enoch was the father of Methuselah, whom the Bible claims lived for 969 years.

With the assumption of Enoch into Heaven there is *a definite parallel* to the life of the prophet Muhammed. There is a tradition that the prophet Muhammed was also taken up into Heaven where he was to meet those prophets who had gone before him. This would profoundly influence the prophet Muhammed because in due course he would call for the commencement of the practice of praying five times daily.

From those Hebrew scriptures designated *Apocryphal* there is *The Book of Enoch* which for a considerable time was thought lost, with only a few fragments remaining. In 1733, however, three copies were brought to the West from Ethiopia.

One of the copies went to *Le Biblioteque du Roi* in Paris and another to *The Bodleian Library* at Oxford.

Muhammed was born in Mecca in or around 570 AD and died on the 8 June 632 AD in Medina.

(21) 'Hic est puer meus *Pimander*, quem ego elegi.'

(22) 'Ipse qui Hermetis mente Pimander erat, in me Christus Ihesus.'

(23) 'Laudabo itaque Iesum Christum sub Pimandri nomine, quad ab Hermete et mens et verbum divinae potentiae interpretatur.'

(24) 'Christianus ego sum, o rex, et Hermeticus simul esse non pudet.'

4: Predisposition; the Only Reality

One of the most contentious issues today is the problem of whether people have what is referred to as *Free Will*, the concern being whether people actually have *a choice* in what they do or how they live their lives in general. Perhaps the answer to this can be found in our history.

All animal and plant life on Earth today are descendants of life forms referred to collectively as the *Protoctista*, more usually referred to as *Protists*. All Protists are single cells. They were the second major life form to appear in the evolutionary process, the first being the Monera.

The Monera are also single cells, but they are much smaller than Protists and much more simple in terms of internal structure. In today's world the Monera are represented by Bacteria.

Let us consider the simplest of life forms, the simplest possible organism. We are not able to communicate with it or them, *any of them*, and their behaviour or their reaction to their situation is in its most elementary form, what we call *reflexive* behaviour. A stimulus is applied and then there is a response; that is all there is.

When life forms became multi-cellular about half-a-billion years ago, cells continued to refine their ability to interpret environmental signals. They also *retained* and improved upon their ability to communicate with each other within the context of a multi-cellular organism; but they did what they did out of *necessity*, not out of choice. Internal clocks profoundly affect behaviour and are to be found in virtually every living organism, whether bacterium, plant or animal.

What could have been the trigger to an evolutionary leap such as some of the *Monera* becoming more complex organisms? It is entirely possible that it was Asteroids which shaped Life's molecules.

Within the evolving Solar System the larger planets may have migrated over considerable distances. The gravitational upheaval of such planetary migration may easily have forced Asteroids out of their home belt between Mars and Jupiter. There may have been a period of considerable displacement about 4 billion years ago when there is a possibility that Jupiter migrated inwards whilst Saturn migrated outwards. Many Asteroids would have headed for the Sun and the inner planets, including Earth. Crater evidence suggests that there was a major Asteroid bombardment approximately 3.9 billion years ago. The Earth has had experience of regular collisions with Space Rocks since then (1).

Yet here we are actually referring to ourselves, are we not? Perhaps the question should be: do we, *as Humans* have a choice? How much of what we do is actual choice, and not just reflexive behaviour?

If we go to the world of Religion there are mixed messages. The author (John Houston) had a reasonably mild religious upbringing, as a Scottish Presbyterian which was greatly influenced by John Calvin, the greatest of second generation Protestant Reformers.

Calvinism's response to the question of whether we have Free Will or not is unambiguous:

> There are those who will grant that this doctrine of *Predestination*, which St. Paul treats here, to be true, for they dare not contradict the Holy Spirit, yet they would that it were buried so that it might never be spoken of. But they merely show themselves to be nothing but fools in controlling the Holy Spirit who spoke it by the prophets and apostles, and even by the mouth of God's only Son. For when our Lord intends to assure us of our salvation, he brings us back to this *eternal election* (2).

By the same token, we could go to the Higher Religion of the Ancient World which was known as Hermetism and consult the Hermetic Tradition to see what it has to say. For the Hermetic Tradition, it was a matter of *natural inclination and Astrology*, none of which are concerned with choice:

> This Knowledge is presented in the *Picatrix* under the form of a revelation made in his sleep to Hermes by Complete Nature. She instructs Hermes as to how she may be invoked by means of the four spirits which compose her and which make possible her operations.
>
> Not all men are, however, capable of possessing this Knowledge; only those who have received a *natural inclination* may aspire to it, through their own virtue and through the disposition of the planets reigning at their nativity.
>
> With the help of Complete Nature, the wise man has the key to open the secrets of the world. Asked what Complete Nature is, Hermes Trismegistus replies: Once the *colligato* or link is established, Complete Nature becomes an Instructress who, by supporting the *natural inclination* of the disciple leads him on to ever higher goals.
>
> The discourse of Complete Nature and her revelation to Hermes has recalled *The Pimander*, with its Revelation of Mind to Hermes and what were the later revelations of Hermes Trismegistus to his disciples (3).

What of contemporary thinkers? Let us consider what Noam Chomsky has to say:

> In spite of all his denials, Chomsky is the most important linguist who has ever lived. "It is hardly an exaggeration to say that there is no major theoretical issue in linguistics today that is debated in terms other than those in which he has chosen to define it," declares *The Encyclopaedia Britannica*. Chomsky's position in the history of ideas has been likened to that of Descartes and Darwin. When Chomsky was in graduate school in the 1950s, linguistics... and all the social sciences was dominated by *Behaviourism*, which hewed to John Locke's notion that the mind begins as a *tabula rasa*, a blank slate that is inscribed upon by experience. Chomsky challenged this approach. He contended that children could not possibly learn language solely

through induction, or trial and error, as *Behaviourists* believed. Some fundamental principles of language… a kind of universal grammar must be embedded in our brains. Chomsky's theories, which he first set forth in his 1957 book, *Syntactic Structures*, helped to rout *Behaviourism* once and for all and paved the way for a more Kantian (4), genetically-orientated view of Human language and cognition. Edward Wilson and other scientists who attempt to explain Human behaviour *in genetic terms* are all, in a sense, indebted to Chomsky (5).

What are the implications of all of this? It means that our lives are *not* our own. We exist for a *purpose* but, unfortunately, *we do not yet know* what that purpose is. How could we find out?

We are now able to freely postulate that there is *no* such thing as Free Will; but people believed it existed, indeed they *wanted to believe* that they had Free Will. Churches proclaimed that people had a choice and they could quote chapter and verse from either the Old or the New Testaments to prove it.

Why should Free Will, whether we view it as a Deception or as a Fantasy, have been proclaimed at all?

The answer is, probably, that it all came down to ethical and, indeed, political expediency. Its aim was to support social harmony and reinforce civil order. It would bolster respect for the Ruling Elite. This gave rise to the Oriental paradox of Free Will and the other part of the equation, *Karma*.

Popular Religion has had a difficult job to do. People, in the vast majority of cases, do *not* frequent Churches or Temples for the sake of Theology; most do so because they are lonely, or they need to alleviate feelings of guilt or anxiety, or even to express authentic religious inclinations.

The Clergy were quite happy to conceal *Determinism* by means of omission. Their concern was to see the congregation as content as possible, thus cheerful and well-behaved. They knew that the inner, *esoteric* or even *occult* beliefs would continue undisturbed and this did not concern them as long as they were kept hidden from view.

Belief in *Karma* was encouraged, the purpose of *The Doctrine of Karma* being supernatural Law enforcement of Law enforcement by means of Superstition.

As stated earlier, this need not be a bad thing. Karma, or *belief in* Karma, would be able to provide a focus for mental and moral effort. It would sustain hope whilst checking malevolence, greed and selfishness and, in some cases, it could motivate self-discipline, aspiration and mercy. These are undoubted benefits.

We see, then, that Karma or Free Will may or may not be true but they have *much to recommend them* as vehicles for moral improvement. At the back of believers' minds there was the realisation that benevolence to those who had been enemies was *supernaturally void* if, even secretly, those former enemies were still hated.

Churches, as we have seen, did not have to do a great deal to discourage the recognition of the superficiality of Free Will. The strength of Religion is that people *want* to believe it and, moreover, belief in Religion is belief in Divine Providence, belief that there is a Supreme Being who has real concern for the Human Race.

The realisation that we are *not* ultimately responsible for our motives or deeds, or our nature, could lead morally or intellectually shallow people to express their worst inclinations by giving bad conduct a most spurious excuse. Here we see why the social consequences of denouncing Free Will could be very unfortunate.

We do make decisions but how we *respond* to the choice, so-called, is *pre-determined*; nonetheless, the Free Will Deception was perpetrated in the interests of social control and common peace.

How can we arrive at a clearer understanding of the Evolutionary Process in which we find ourselves? For the author (John Houston) it is about understanding *Predisposition*, and that it is Predisposition that makes everything possible, being the cause of everything. It is Predisposition which is seeking to *create an Identity*, an Identity which will permit Predisposition full Self-Expression.

It can be understood as follows; Predisposition *requires* Consciousness for Self-Experience and Self-Expression. The Human Race is the *personalisation* of Divine Predisposition. By means of the Human Race, Predisposition becomes conscious of Itself in a personal manner.

In centuries now gone when the Human Race was described within the prophetic communities as *the source of all Wisdom and Power*, we can understand this as implying that the Human Race has been created by Predisposition, the Predisposition which is seeking to provide *an identity for God*. In other words, by means of Humanity, God as Divine Identity can be created. This is *why* the Human Race exists.

For God, the Predisposition to be God *has to be incarnated* or there is non-Identity. Incarnation is therefore inevitable. God, as Divine Identity, is *predestined* in as much as God is *predisposed to become* fully God.

This is a Process, a Process which has as its Purpose *the personalisation* of the Predisposition to *be* God. This is Incarnation, the *becoming* of a Person. Incarnation is about the Revelation of Divine Identity. It is also the activation of Racial Memory.

Our Predisposition is about Recollection for the Divine Gnosis that comes *as* Recollection. The Human Race exists to remember or, in other words, the Human Race exists to make such Recollection *possible*. The 'what we have to remember' is being personalised to become the *Manifestation* of the Divine Self, God and Self to Infinite Complexity. The Human Race is *the consciousness* of the Divine Predisposition to be God, refined, and potentially perfected.

What more can be said about this? The Eternal Predisposition to *be* God is *personalised as the Human Race*. By means of Human Consciousness the Original Predisposition to be the Godhead can be Remembered and, subsequently, *Reborn*. This is the same thing as saying that God has acquired the Divine Identity for God has been *limited to Form* for the sake of *acquiring* an Identity for Manifestation, indeed *Incarnation*.

It is the Acquisition of the Divine Identity which makes everything possible for God. The quest for Identity is the key to attainment. Before the beginning of the process which we call Life, there was non-Identity, *no one* to become. That which is Allness and Absolute was no more than an Abstraction.

The sub-personalities of the Godhead *must* exist in order that the Supreme Personality of Godhead can be revealed. This is Hermes, this is Ion, the Son of Apollo, intent upon revealing Himself. Through Rebirth *beyond* the Human stage as we understand it, the Supreme Personality of Godhead can further *assume* the Identity of the Original Predisposition to be God, for the Supreme Personality of Godhead, whether we refer to this Person as either Hermes or Ion, *is the Identity* of that Original Predisposition.

Containment, as Form, is for the sake of personalisation which entails the Acquisition of Identity. Predisposition comes to know Itself by means of what It has created *unconsciously*. Containment is for personalisation which leads to the Acquisition of Identity because Predisposition requires it. All Creation is the Creation of Self, *as* Identity.

Pythagoras stated that what gives *Form* to *The Unlimited* is none other than *The Limit*. This *Limit* is Predisposition with this *Limit* being the potential for the *manifestation* of God in terms of *Predisposition*.

It is about Predisposition with a process of personalisation for the sake of the Acquisition of Identity; this Identity exists for the sake of the Predisposition which *requires* it.

All Creation is the Creation of our history, of *how* we came into being, for the purpose of Life is that we be *created*. Creation is therefore the Creation of History, with History being the record of the outworking of Predisposition. The History of the Mind is the History of the outworking of the Predisposition of the Mind, the Predisposition which made the Creation of Mind possible, indeed *unavoidable*.

The Knowledge or Gnosis which we seek, which comes *as* Recollection, is Knowledge concerning Predisposition. When ignorance is removed there is *no* barrier to the realisation of Predisposition.

All we need to know now is our Predisposition. There would be nothing at all but for the Predisposition to *become* God.

Life is necessary due to Predisposition; indeed Predisposition has life as Its *Necessity*. Order will always triumph because of Predisposition.

Life personalises Predisposition and it is the Consciousness of Predisposition which evolves; as such each Human being is a relationship of Sensory Perception for the sake of the *self-expression* of the Predisposition which we are and for which we exist.

Inclination is the manifestation of Predisposition for it is as Inclination that Predisposition expresses Itself. Predisposition is the *sensation* of Self; indeed Self-Expression is *unavoidable* because of Predisposition.

By means of the Human Race, Predisposition can experience *purpose* for Humanity can become the *Will* of Predisposition. We are the personalising of the Will of the Predisposition to *be* God.

This is Pre-Existence, where Identity is to be *attained*; in the state of Pre-Existence the only possibility is Predisposition.

Because Life has been characterised by *Containment* which is, itself, for the purpose of *the Acquisition of Identity*, there is something of paramount importance to be realised here. By means of the Human Race the Universal is able to express Itself through *Particulars*.

In general terms, Religion, to date, has hinted that the purpose of God is to go from expression by means of Particulars *to* the Universal; this is actually incorrect. Particulars are *not* seeking to become Universals.

Although Human beings exist to give expression to the Will of *The Infinite*, that Infinity of God can only be expressed by *Finite* means. The Human Race can only express *The Infinite* by means of *the Finiteness* of the evolving Human Form.

Particulars, *as Limit,* which provide Form for *The Unlimited* or Formless, have as their purpose the *expression* of *The Unlimited* or Universal *as* Identity. Without Particulars this would be impossible.

The process is the Creation of Self, the Universal Self. The outcome of the process is Self-Expression and the purpose of the process is the *continuation* of Self.

From Allness and Absolute the Godhead, *as* the expression of Predisposition and by means of Containment, has created an Identity by means of Particulars. It happened this way out of Necessity.

The Universe exists *as* the outworking of the Predisposition to be or to become God; this Predisposition has to do with the Creation of a Collective Consciousness which the Ultimate Ancestor may use for the expression of Its Reproduction.

This is the status of the Human Race; we exist for the propagation of the Ultimate Ancestor because *if* the Ultimate Ancestor can utilise Humanity *as* the Divine Identity then it means that, thereby, the Ultimate Ancestor can *assume* Human form. This sets the stage for what is therefore rendered possible because now the Ultimate Ancestor can reproduce Itself; simultaneously the Human Race becomes further *Deified.*

NOTES

(1)   *Sky at Night Magazine.* From the BBC May 2009 Edition www.skyatnightmagazine.com. From *News,* edited by Hazel Muir. See page 10.

> Asteroids played a crucial role in the shaping of the molecules of life on Earth. A new study of meteorites suggests that ancient watery asteroids preferentially stockpiled 'left-handed' amino acid molecules before crashing into our planet, biasing pre-biotic chemistry so that it favoured left-handed proteins…
>
> Life uses 20 amino acid molecules to build millions of different proteins, the workhouse molecules of life. Amino acids exist in

two mirror-image forms: right-handed and left-handed. Newly evolving life had to opt for one or the other...

Almost every organism on Earth uses left-handed amino acids. So what made life choose left over right? Meteorites might hold the answer. Tests in the 1990s revealed that they contain an excess of left-handed amino acids of up to 15 per cent. This bias could have arisen because polarised starlight passing through the Solar System preferentially destroyed right-handed amino acids, leaving more lefties behind.

However, it was unclear how polarised starlight could create such a strong bias. Now Glavin and Dworkin have shown that another factor is water, which flowed on some asteroids millions of years ago. "Radioactive heating in the interiors of asteroids provided enough heat to melt their ice and do very interesting chemistry..." The team studied an amino acid called *isovaline* in six meteorites, including the famous Murchison meteorite.

The rocks are thought to have been exposed to water for around 1,000 to 10,000 years.

The longer the water persised in the rock, the stronger its left-handed *isovaline* bias... "This gives us a hint that the creation of extra left-handed amino acids had something to do with alteration by water."

The likelihood is that something – possibly polarised starlight – created a small left-handed bias in amino acids in water on asteroid surfaces. Right- and left-handed forms crystallised out of the solution in equal measure, sticking together in pairs. Polarised light continued creating an excess of lefties in the water as more pairs solidified out, amplifying the bias.

After asteroids delivered their organic cargo to Earth, left-handed proteins became life's easiest option.

(2) John Calvin, *Sermons on the Epistle to the Ephesians*. Published by *The Banner of Truth Trust*, 1998 reprint, page 25.

Calvinism is based upon the belief that there is an elect group who are to inherit the Kingdom of Heaven. These people have been chosen for such, something which many people find difficult about Calvinism, that there is *no* choice in life. Those who become Christians, with these being the people who will survive the Day of Judgement, are those who have been chosen *by* God.

This is why we read in *The Acts of the Apostles* such as "and the Lord added daily to the Church such as *should* be saved". In *The Epistle of Paul to the Romans*, we read that "God has mercy on whom God has mercy, God has compassion on whom God has compassion". Some vessels are *destined* for honour whilst others are destined for dishonour, not through personal choice but by the *will* of God.

(3) *Marsilio Ficino and the Return of Hermes Trismegistus.* Published jointly by *The Biblioteca Medicea Laurenziana* in Florence and *The Bibliotheca Philosophica Hermetica*, in Amsterdam in 1999, page 110.

(4) Immanuel Kant, the greatest of Metaphysicians was born on 22 April 1724 in Konigsberg, the principal town of East Prussia. His influence caused the greatest revolution which Metaphysical Science had ever experienced.

His father, John George Kant, was a saddler in Konigsberg, the son of a Scotsman who had lived in Aberdeenshire, in Scotland, until the end of the seventeenth century when not a few Scots made their way to the Baltic shores. Nothing is known of the grandfather whose name was originally Cant.

It was said of Immanuel Kant that he had inherited the stern integrity of his Scottish Presbyterian Ancestors tempered by the affectionate piety of his mother, Anna Regina Reuter, a genuine German.

Kant introduced a *Theory of Cosmic Evolution* which, at the time, was a whole new way of considering Reality. The existing moulds of Thought were shattered because Kant's *Doctrine of the Ideality of the World* undermined those beliefs which saw the world as firmly grounded in Space and Time.

For Kant, if there is any value which does have value, it must lie outside the whole sphere of what *happens*; it must lie *outside* the world.

The empirical world had never, at the level of Intuition, been taken by Richard Wagner as the *whole* of Reality.

(5) John Horgan, *The End of Science*, Published in the USA by *Addison-Wesley* in 1996 and in the UK by *Little, Brown & Company*, in 1997. From the chapter, *The End of Social Science*, page 151.

5: Plato

Plato, a name which is derived from the Greek *platon*, which means *the broad one*, was the most celebrated philosopher of Antiquity. He was born in the year 429 BC, either in Athens or on the neighbouring island of Aegina.

Plato's lineage was ancient as well as being illustrious. It ascended on his father's side to Kodros and on his mother's side to Solon. His original name of *Aristokles* was to give way to *Plato*, either on account of the *broadness* of his shoulders, or else the *comprehensiveness* of his genius.

Fable was to throw her marvels around his infancy. One day his parents had gone to Mount Hymettus where they would make sacrifice to the Nymphs and Graces. Nearby the young Plato was asleep on a bower of myrtles and, as he lay there, a swarm of bees is said to have alighted harmlessly on his lips. It has been suggested that this ingenious fancy was an indicator of the sweetness of his literary style.

When Plato was twenty he would meet his great mentor, Socrates. This was an event too remarkable to remain unembellished by marvellous accompaniments.

The night previous to their meeting Socrates had had a dream. He saw a young swan flying towards him from an altar in the Groves of Akademos. It was to rest briefly upon the bosom of the wise Socrates, after which it was to soar up beyond the clouds. Then, Socrates was later to claim, he heard strains of music *so powerful* that it could all too easily have ravished the souls of both gods and mere mortals such as ourselves.

The philosophy of Plato is usually and conveniently divided into three sections; these sections were Dialectic (sometimes known as *Metaphysics*), Physics and Ethics.

In Ethics he was to follow the principles of Socrates. As for Physics, he was to borrow from much older Cosmogonies. In Dialectic Plato is *eminently original*; indeed Dialectic is Plato's peculiar contribution to Science. *Dialectic is the Science of Ideas.* What then are *Ideas*?

Firstly, we must state the opinion which *The Theory of Ideas* was designed to correct or supplement. It may be assumed as a general rule in philosophy that every new Doctrine has for its object the *correction* either of some antecedent scientific error or of some natural *oversight* incident to ordinary thinking. In order to fully understand a new Doctrine we should first of all understand the old opinion to which it was opposed.

In this case the old system was known as *Sensationalism* which resolved all thought and knowledge into *Sensation*. The purport of *The Platonic Theory*, on the other hand, is that in the constitution of Knowledge, *Sensation* is only a part and *not* the highest part. For Plato the light of our Knowledge comes from Ideas, *not* Sensation (1).

For Plato, all general conceptions, such as *man, animal* or *tree*, are Ideas. They are also called Universals, to distinguish them from the *Particulars* which are included under them. According to Plato, the first stage of Knowledge is *not* the apprehension of Particulars but the apprehension of Ideas and Universals (2) and the *application* of these *to* Particulars.

For Plato, there is an actual *abstract* man as well as the individual and concrete man known as Charles, Edward or Jonathan. The latter can *only* be known by the *apprehension* of the former (3).

This apprehension is possible because of the *immortality* of the soul which has been conscious of *the pure Ideas* in its previous state, *before birth*. This permits us to *recognise* things from their likeness to the heavenly *Ideas*.

Plato conceived of a whole world of *Ideas*, as he called them. Before birth, according to Plato, our souls live among *the Absolute*, which is the absolutely beautiful, the absolutely true, the absolutely just. Then, in this world, we see things which are *partly* beautiful, *partly* true, *partly* just and we *remember* those *antenatal* perceptions and this permits us to *recognise* what, in terms of planet Earth, are what we call beautiful things, true thoughts and just actions.

These partake in a partial and imperfect way of those great, perfect Universals, the knowing of which is the *only real Knowledge*; indeed these are the only Realities which remain steadfast among the shifting phenomena of life.

We are conscious in a mysterious sense of having seen a thing before which all evidence tends to suggest we are seeing for the first time. This is an experience extended to every part of the Mind. Many feel that they have lived before, for example, and with Wordsworth they declare:

> Our birth is but a sleep and a forgetting;
> The soul that rises with us,
> Our life's star,
> Hath had somewhere else its setting
> And cometh from afar.

For Plato, *The Theory of Ideas* makes Knowledge to *originate* in Ideas; for Plato it is incorrect to assert that Ideas come from Knowledge.

The Platonic Theory can be summed up by saying that the Mind thinks and knows by means of *Genera* and *Species*. They are the *essential* conditions for *all* thought, *all* knowledge and *all* existence. It is impossible for a thing to either exist or to be known to exist, except as an instance of some Genus or Species.

According to Plato, therefore, Genera and Species, which are actually *Ideas*, are the most objective, the most independent, the most real and the most enduring of all things in as much as they are the *necessary* laws and principles on which *all* being and *all* knowledge are dependent.

Those who are *Platonist* in outlook would hold that the Mind has truths *implanted* in it *beyond* experience. Leibniz stated that *The Doctrine of Innate Ideas* teaches not so much that the actual norms of space, time, cause, number and form, right and wrong, God and immortality are as such *already* in the mind at birth but, rather, that the *capacity* is there.

The fact that *the capacity* is there is just another way of saying that there is *a Predisposition* seeking to express itself. This is why people come into the world *already equipped* to do something with excellence.

This may be what Plato meant when we read in *The Phaedrus*, "...the self-moving is the beginning of motion; and this can neither be destroyed nor begotten..." (4).

NOTES

(1) From the writings of Plato and, in this case from *The Theaetetus*, we learn that the actual purpose of *The Theaetetus* is to clear the ground by showing that Knowledge cannot be identified either with Sensation or with Thought.

(2) *The Dialogues of Plato*. Translated by J. Harward. Published by *The Encyclopaedia Britannica, Inc.* Sixth Printing in 1996. From *The Phaedrus*, page 126.

> For man must have intelligence of Universals, and be able to proceed from the many Particulars of sense to one conception of Reason: this is the recollection of those things which our soul once saw while following God when, regardless of that which we now call being she raised her head up towards the *true* being. And therefore the mind of the philosopher alone has wings; and this is just, for He is always, according to the measure of His abilities, clinging in recollection to those things in which God abides, and in the beholding of which He is what He is. And He who employs aright these memories is ever being *initiated into Perfect Mysteries* and alone becomes truly perfect.

(3) Since there is only *one* Reality, which has to do with the *outworking* of Predisposition, the *truth* of any given situation is that Predisposition is being *expressed*. The actual *abstract man* mentioned here is *how* a person is *predisposed* for, until the Creation of an Identity to express Predisposition, that Predisposition is no more than *an abstraction*.

The concrete man, so to speak, is a *mere phenomenon*, whereas it is his Predisposition which is the only Reality conceived here.

(4) as (2) above. See page 124.

> And therefore the self-moving is the beginning of motion; and this can neither be destroyed nor begotten, else the whole heavens and all creation would collapse and stand still, and never again have motion or birth. But if the self-moving is proved to be immortal, he who affirms that self-motion is the very idea and essence of the soul will not be put to confusion.

6: Ion, the Son of Apollo

I

Ion was the mythical Ancestor of the Ionians, a people of Ancient Greece. It was generally accepted that his father was none other than the god Apollo, the Master Musician. His mother was *Kreousa*, sometimes *Creusa*, the wife of Xouthos, the King of Athens and elsewhere. Apollo had met Kreousa in a cave below the Akropolis.

Sometime later Kreousa had hoped for another visit from Apollo. She had gone to the cave where she had met Apollo before and, with her, she had her infant son, *Ion*. She had hoped to gain protection for her infant son from her god lover.

Apollo did not appear, however; she departed from the cave leaving her young son behind her. It was then that Apollo made his appearance and in due course he was to convey the child to the Temple at Delphi, where the young boy grew up as the youth Ion, surrounded by priestesses.

Years later, Xouthos, the King of Athens, *being childless*, decided to go to the Temple at Delphi in order that he might *consult the Oracle*; whilst at the Temple he was duly informed that upon leaving the Precincts of the Temple the first youth he meets will be his son.

Xouthos was to meet Ion and he was truly overjoyed because his tale would appear to have acquired a happy ending. No doubt he wondered *why* things had been the way they had been and one night he was to confess to Kreousa he thought he was beginning to understand the mystery and that he was convinced that there had been *key moments* in his own childhood and manhood which could explain everything, thus putting things into their proper context.

For one reason or another Kreousa was enraged by his confession for Ion was *her* son. It was then that she decided *to murder Ion* by giving him a poisonous drink. Good fortune was to prevail, however, and Ion was to discover the trap and survive.

He had met Kreousa and was offered a libation for his refreshment, upon which he was to piously pour out a few drops. A pigeon drank of the libation as it lay on the ground and it died instantly.

As we might expect Ion was horrified by this, rushing upon the would-be murderess to kill her, *but he did not*. Mother and son had been made known to each other. Xouthos was to receive Ion as his own son whilst Kreousa *kept her secret*.

Ion was to become the founder of *the Ionians*, a people who originated within the Hellenic Race. The historian Herodotus says of the Athenians that they were *Pelasgoi* (1) but that they took the name Ionians from *Ion*, the son of Xouthos. The name only appears once in *The Iliad* in the form of *Iaones*.

Their influence was to grow considerably and, ultimately, there would be a Confederation of Ionian Cities. The Confederation was united by common religious worship and the Celebration of certain periodic Festivals. The place of assembly was the Panionium, at the foot of Mount Mukale where there was a Temple dedicated to Poseidon (2).

There are *no* materials for the construction of a history of any *political union* of these Ionian cities; yet wherever Ionians settled the inhabitants became wealthy, prosperity being their aim. They had a great taste for the Arts and their Temples and public buildings were to rival those of European Greece. The Ionian Religion had splendid and elaborate Ceremonies.

The Temple of Artemis in Ephesus was famous throughout Antiquity, being *one of the wonders of the world*. The rich trading Ionian cities were luxurious and refined beyond anything conceived by their European relatives. The fine Ionian Order of Architecture was due to them; the earliest and grandest School of Greek Painting was also theirs.

The Literature of Greece may be said to have originated with the Ionians. The historian Hecateus was a native of Miletos; Thales, one of the earliest philosophers, was from the same country; Anacreon, one of the most famous lyric poets from Antiquity, was a native of Teos; Herodotus, the historian, although a Dorian, adopted the language of his Ionian neighbours (3).

Then there was *The Ionian School of Philosophy*, something which is of interest to us, even today as we shall see in due course. At the very least *The Ionian School of Philosophy* comprises several of the earliest philosophers of Greece. These chief Ionian philosophers were Thales, Anaximines, Anaximander of Miletos, Pythagoras of Samos, Xenophanes of Kolophon, Heraclitus of Ephesus and Anaxagorus of Klazomenai.

The general tendency of Ionian philosophy was *the investigation* of Matter. Ionian philosophers sought for that *root-principle* which demonstrated the union of Life *with* Matter. For the Ionians, Matter was Nature and it had an in-built vitality. Life was deemed to be inseparably connected with Matter.

The Ionians had a great love of Music. This is hardly surprising since the real father of Ion was Apollo, who was a fabulous Musician.

Pythagoras was of great importance in the growth of the Western Philosophical Tradition. He revered Apollo more than any other god. Disciples of Pythagoras were apt to use Medicine to purge the body and Music to purge the soul, the purgative function of Music being fully recognised in the Psychotherapy of those days. Some say this practice was derived from the Korybantic Priests who used Music to treat nervous and hysterical patients.

Socrates, the wisest man in the ancient world, believed that "Music was the highest philosophy" and that, like a dying swan, with his final breath he would sing out in praise of Apollo.

II

We need to know why this is of relevance to us today. We have mentioned Pythagoras, who was an Ionian, and a landmark in philosophy. Prior to Pythagoras the general view of the world was *Milesian* in character. Herodotus, the Ionian, stated that these Milesians were "pertaining to the Irish or Scottish Race". Here, at the very least, there is an association with Gaeldom.

Bards from the Scottish Highlands maintained that the Scots had become known as such after their leader, Milesius, had married Scota, the daughter of an Egyptian Pharaoh; thus the Ancient Scots were *connected* to the Milesians whose influence upon us has been colossal, just as the Scottish nation *as we know it now* has had a colossal influence upon the Human Race, especially over the last four centuries with the advent of the British Empire.

Miletos was the most southerly of the twelve Ionian cities. It had been *the focus* for literature and philosophy. Thales, the founder of Milesian Cosmology, lived there. Other philosophers such as Anaximander and Anaximines did also; indeed Anaximander was to succeed Thales as the leader of *The Milesian Tradition*.

Anaximander held that all life began in the sea and that the *present form* of animals was the result of *adaptation* to a fresh environment. Recognising that the young of the Human Race require a prolonged period of nursing whereas the young of other species soon find food for themselves, led Anaximander to conclude that if Humans had *always* been as they are now they would *not* have been able to survive (4).

The greatest contribution of all by the Milesians to Human knowledge was their concept of *Matter*; with *The Fall of Miletos* in 494 BC, it is generally accepted that the Milesian School of Philosophy came to an end.

But was it really the end? Those Milesians were to continue their existence in association with the Ancient Scottish nation. These Ancient Scots had their own view of the world, a view which was syncretistic, and in due course they had to forsake Ireland, which had been known as *Scotia*, to establish a Scots colony in Pictland, which was to become known as Scotland (5). This was around 500 AD.

There was no going back. The religious leader of the Scots, Saint Columba (6), sought to create a religious establishment in the new Scots colony known as *Dal Riada*.

The Ancient Scots had been influenced by Ancient Egypt as well as the Milesians and then the Ionians among others yet, by the time that the religious community was founded in what would become known as *Scotland*, it would appear that the greatest influence upon the Ancient Scots was the philosophy of the Ionians. It is for this reason that when the religious centre of the Ancient Scots was established it was to appear on an island known as *Iona* (7).

The author (John Houston) was brought up to believe that Saint Columba had brought Christianity to Scotland and that this *true* Christian Faith had subsequently been *undermined*, having been *Romanised* and altered beyond all recognition. It appears, yet further, to the author (John Houston) that these true *Christian Mysteries*, of which the Ancient Scots had become the

Supreme Custodians, were *not* founded upon Jesus Christ at all but upon *Ion*, the mythical son of Apollo.

When we look at maps of the Western Isles of Scotland and elsewhere, there is evidence of there having been Temples. These Temples were dedicated to *Ion*, the Sun god and mythical Son of Apollo (8).

Here we see the legacy of Gaeldom and as we approach a New Age, the true and complete Renaissance which will hold the key to the attainment of Human Destiny. What should we expect to happen?

On one level, it will be the *resurrection* of the British Empire, which existed *for the Scots*, so that they might be scattered throughout the world until such time as they would emerge as *guides* to the Human Race, which is their Destiny.

On another level it will be the reinstatement of *The True Religion* of the Human Race, which is that which was proclaimed by the Ionians and, thereafter, the Scots among the other nations of the Earth which is: the *true* Son of God is none other than *Ion*, the Son of Apollo.

NOTES

(1) Herodotus, *The Histories*, VIII. 44.

(2) The twelve Ionian cities were: Phokaia, the most northerly; Klazomenai; Chios; Euthrai; Teos; Lebedos; Kolophon; Ephesus; Samos in Lydia; Priene; Muous; and Miletos, the most southerly, in Karia.

Smyrna, being seized by Kolophonian exiles, was added to the Confederation in 700 BC.

(3) Herodotus, *The Histories*. From *The Introduction*, page xix.

Not much is known of the life of Herodotus and the few items that have come down to us are not above suspicion. A late source, the eleventh-century Byzantine Lexicon known as *The Suda*, preserves a number of biographical details: that Herodotus was born in Halicarnassus, the son of Lyxes and Dryo, and the brother of Theodorus: that he was the nephew or cousin of an Epic poet, Panyassis, who wrote on historical themes, such as the founding of the Ionian cities: that he was exiled by the tyrant of

Halicarnassus, Lygdamis, to the Isle of Samos, where he learned the Ionian dialect of Greek in which his *Histories* is composed: that he afterwards returned to Halicarnassus, assisting in expelling Lygdamis and then, seeing himself hated by his fellow citizens, went into exile and joined in the foundation of Thurii, an Athenian-led pan-Hellenic colony in Southern Italy: and that he died there or perhaps in Macedonia at Pella.

(4) We have no idea of the extent of knowledge at their disposal. They certainly knew about *evolution* or so it seems, long before the time of Charles Darwin.

(5) The ancient name for Scotland is *Caledonia*; it was also known as *Pictland*, as it was dominated by the Picts, who are usually depicted as P Celtic, or *Brythonic*.

(6) Saint Columba was known as *Colm Cille* and in Gaidhlig (Gaelic). Iona was known as *I Colm Cille*.

Saint Columba founded the establishment in 563 AD. It was an establishment of *Culdees*. They were not subject to vows but were governed by a Code of Laws formed by Saint Columba. It was to continue for centuries having acquired the highest reputation for sanctity and learning.

The remains of forty-eight Scottish kings, four Irish kings and eight Norwegian kings are to be found on Iona.

(7) Why would the island where the religious establishment of *The Culdees* was situated be referred to as *Iona*, were it not for *the honouring of Ion* by a community which was determined to make a fresh start in their new homeland? Perhaps they felt that it was their duty, their calling, to display to others that they revered Ion, the Son of Apollo, above *all* others.

(8) From *The Dialogues of Plato*, we read of cheerful interplay between Ion and Socrates.

Here is an example from page 142:

Socrates: "Welcome Ion. Are your from your native city of Ephesus?"

Ion: "No, Socrates; but from Epidaurus, where I attended *The Festival of Asclepius*."

Socrates: "And do the Epidaurians have contests of rhapsodes at the Festival?"

Ion: "O yes; and all sorts of musical performers."

Socrates: "And were you one of the competitors? And did you succeed?"

Ion: "I obtained first prize of all, Socrates."

Socrates: "Well done; and I hope that you will do the same for us at Panathenaea."

Ion: "And I will, please Heaven."

Ion and Socrates continue to share views on important matters. Socrates has already pointed out that all good poets, Epic as well as Lyric, compose their beautiful poems not by Art, but because they are *inspired and possessed.*

Ion replies that there is a difference between the two alternatives. He says he considers Inspiration to be by far the nobler.

Socrates continues by saying that he will assume the nobler alternative and that he will attribute to Ion in his praises of Homer that Ion is guided by *Inspiration* and *not* Art.

7: Prophecy on Subway Walls

I

We are living at a time of unprecedented change for the Human Race. An Old Age – and with it the Old World Order of a Humanity divided against Itself – is due to disappear and will soon be gone forever; but who or what will replace it? The answer is a New World Order which is coming, indeed a New World Order whose appearance has been *foretold*, for its appearance is *predestined*.

Such a New World Order is necessary for several reasons. In the first instance someone *has* to take responsibility for what happens and, accordingly, someone *has* to police the world. What would any community be like without a police force to *enforce* law and order, especially in the world as it is at present, where *not all* the leaders are altruistic and where the greatest profits have come from *organised corruption*? Who could *realistically* fulfil such a role dealing with rogue states in defence of the moral majority?

Then there is the question of water or, more correctly, the certain *shortage* of water because of the changing rainfall patterns. We are approaching the time when people all over the planet will be adversely affected by *serious* water shortage.

Those asylum seekers we see now may prove to be no more than the tip of the proverbial iceberg, a foretaste of what lies in store for us. *If* the well runs dry, so to speak, it may well mean that millions and millions of people will be uprooted as the glaciers, the rivers and the lochs which have sustained towns and cities do a disappearing act.

Millions and millions could well be wiped out by drought and the famine and pestilence which will come as an accompaniment. Then there will be the effect of nations defending their frontiers against wave after relentless wave of people desperate to find stability and security where they can build a life for themselves and for their families.

At this time, the collapse of the present World Order is becoming more self-evident; indeed the world of monetary economics has now gone into freefall. After this the problems really will start to escalate. This was hinted at in February 2001 when *The Intergovernmental Panel on Climate Change* stated that "environments are going to change much more severely than was thought".

It is *no* exaggeration to assert that we are living in uncertain times, living as we do at a time when an Old Age is in terminal decline; the *need* for us to adapt our communal lifestyle to comply with the *demands* made upon us by the approach of a New Age will become more and more apparent. Old certainties are disappearing and no one seems to be able to do a thing about it. Yet behind everything there is an *underlying* trend for all to see! What might that be?

As it happens, 2003 was the four hundredth anniversary of the Union of the Crowns, the event which heralded the birth of the British Empire with the subsequent appearance of nations such as Canada, the United States of America, South Africa, Australia and New Zealand among others.

Could it be that we are about to witness the *further* unfolding of an *Ancient Saga* whose last chapter began four centuries ago? On 5 March 1603, James VI, King of Scots and son of Mary, Queen of Scots, left Scotland for London where, on the 24 March 1603, he became James I, King of Great Britain and Ireland.

James I, King of Great Britain and Ireland, *the Monarch of the Thistle and the Rose,* was to see the beginnings of the largest, most powerful and yet the most *liberal* Empire the world had ever seen. This was an Empire which was *predestined* and its founders accepted this (1).

One thing is certain; our mounting problems are *global* in extent and, if they are to be tackled effectively, they have to be tackled on a *global* basis. Global Cooperation for the sake of protecting the environment can only take place when it has first been decided who *rules* on a *global* basis.

We must ask ourselves a question; as the response to the Iraqi situation unfolded with action led by the United States of America and the United

Kingdom, was it *mere coincidence* that it took place *exactly* 400 years after the Union of the Crowns which heralded the *birth* of the British Empire (2)?

Our history bids us recognise and revere the bonds which link the British Isles with the rest of the English-speaking world. Should there be a Rebirth or Reawakening of British Culture, then it will not be restricted to the British Isles as was the case in 1603.

As far as the author (John Houston) is concerned, the British Empire must rise again as the Commonwealth, to which the United States of America (karmically British) will be restored. Therein, the United States of America with the other English-speaking nations could lead the other nations of the Earth to the establishment of a global Commonwealth *family* of nations based on the understanding that the Human Race is *One*.

The English-speaking nations, with others, must now create a New World Order based on the English language and, in going *beyond* Protestantism, establish *The Kingdom of God* on Earth, a state of affairs which has been *foretold* by those whom we recognise as having had prophetic insight (3).

Within this New World Order the Scots will be the Royal Nation; indeed it is *the will of God* that the Scots should rule the Earth, which is their Destiny, as has been revealed to me (John Houston), having been endowed by God with *prophetic* insight.

Come what may, a New World Order, indeed a New Age will appear from the ashes of the Old Age and from the approaching Tribulation, a period of chaos with severe consequences. This is how the planet Earth, as a Super Organism, gets things done. Accordingly, this is hardly a new thing because, when we examine the fossil records, we see that there have been mass extinction events on Earth. The purpose is the increased *quality* of the surviving species.

There are mass extinction peaks 65 million years ago, which marked the end for the Dinosaurs (4), then 39 million years ago and 13 million years ago; that is, every 26 million years.

> For the Dinosaurs, ammonites, and lots of other groups, life ended after an event that happened in Mexico one warm Spring day. We know it was a Spring day because a magnolia flower was found in the wreckage. A chunk of rock from outer space, twenty km in diameter, had hit the Earth off the Yucatan peninsula in South-East Mexico (5).

There is more for:

It appears that mass extinction events happen at different times for different reasons and with very different severity and effect. We know that each event is different and none can be predicted; nevertheless they do have things in common. The events are triggered by environmental changes, possibly from fire and flood, so reducing light and oxygen to slow down photosynthesis and respiration on land and in the sea. The consequent culls usually lead to vacant ecological niches which are eventually occupied by new forms that have adapted to the fresh conditions (6).

This has led to the belief in what is a New Idea, which is *self-organised mass extinction* from within.

Since the Industrial Revolution there has been a distinct third phase, our continuing destruction of the natural environment. Most of what we hear about climate change and global warming can be ascribed to this human activity, though of course some of it is a consequence of natural cycles such as sunspots and other rhythmic processes outside the Earth.

There is another argument that catastrophes such as human-induced environmental changes are a *necessary* feature of the *self-controlled system of life* on earth. As with the avalanches in the sand-pile, they happen when the system reaches a critical state and passes over the edge from one kind of world to another. Equally extinctions are an *essential stimulus* to the evolutionary process. We know this from the patterns that show up in our curves of evolution from the fossil record (7).

II

In these days it is somewhat unfashionable to suggest that people or nations aren't equal; the truth is that some nations are more advanced than others, some are more liberal than others and some are more powerful than others.

At this time the United States of America is by far the most powerful nation on Earth and, for someone who accepts that everything is *pre-destined*, the supremacy of the United States of America has its basis in the *will* of God.

The fact that some nations are more powerful than others has always provoked considerable debate among people.

> We have abundant evidence from the doctrine upheld by Kallikles, namely, that Might is Right, was current in Athens towards the close of the fifth century BC. In *The Melian Dialogue*, Thucydides has shown us how it might be used to justify the attitude of the imperial democracy to its subject allies, and *The Herakles* of Euripides is a study of the same problem.
>
> Its theme is that the strong man is not sufficient to himself, and is only safe so long as he uses his strength in the service of Mankind. This conception of *the strong man* (of which Herakles was the regular type) was not in itself an ignoble one. It had its ideal side, and Pindar sings how Herakles took the oxen of Geryones without paying for them in virtue of that higher law, which "justifies even the most violent deed with a high hand", a passage duly quoted in Plato's *Gorgias*.
>
> Such theories are a natural reaction against that rooted jealousy of everything above the common which is apt to characterise democracy. In modern times Carlyle and Nietzsche represent the same point of view. The worship of the strong man or *hero* who can rise superior to all petty moral conventions, in fact, *the Superman* seems to have been fostered in the fifth century BC by much the same influences as in the nineteenth century AD. It is clear, then, that even the doctrine of Kallikles is not complete ethical nihilism. Might really is Right. That is a very different thing from saying that Right is Might (8).

Neither the Western Philosophical Tradition nor the Sacred Literature from India question the right of a certain *class* or *caste* of people to operate as having *the entitlement of authority over others*. For the Greek philosophers and for the Brahmins of India the existence of a Ruling Caste was viewed as *natural* and not the cause of wonder. It is for this reason that slavery was never truly questioned. This does not mean, however, that those in a position of authority can be abusive or tyrannical. Having the Law on their side they were to be *obeyed* and had the *right* to be obeyed (9).

There are those who have the ability to create employment opportunities for others because they have sufficient initiative, self-discipline and determination to see an idea brought to fruition. There are also others who are *reliant* upon someone else to provide them with employment and they are happy to work *for* someone else.

As Civilisation has appeared bit by bit on the planet we see with the Roman Empire, among others, that slavery was *fundamental* to the economic system. When the Christian Faith was coming into existence some Christians *were* slaves whilst other Christians *owned* slaves.

We know from the Bible that there were guidelines for the protection of slaves. A slave could not be maimed. Women slaves could be taken as wives but they were not to be used by their masters for the sake of sexual gratification. The gist of the Law within Israel was that slaves were to be treated with respect and that it was wrong to abuse them. The slave had inalienable Human rights (10).

Within the early Christian Church *(The Cult of Jesus Christ)*, the Apostle Paul had to deal with the case of a man called Onesimus, a runaway slave who had become a Christian. The Apostle Paul exhorts the Christian master of Onesimus to receive his slave back, *not* just as a slave but "as a brother in Christ" (11).

Neither the Faith of Israel nor the Christian Faith considered slavery to be wrong in and of itself, but rather as demonstrating that there is a *natural* order which is also *hierarchical*. We know that the Western Philosophical Tradition states openly that "a ruling class is indispensable". Plato did not proclaim equality but that "Human ills would not cease until either philosophers became rulers or rulers became philosophers".

What can this possibly mean for us today with the Old World Order collapsing? *Who* will be able to come through the trials and the tribulations to land safely on the other side?

We bear in mind that the *future* Kingdom is *predestined* and that people are actually *predisposed*. Those who will make it through will be those who have *the natural inclination* which equips them to recognise true guidance and thereby *follow* true leadership.

Not so many years ago the author (John Houston) used to do some freelance writing. One of the most interesting and, indeed, one of the most financially rewarding commissions was to produce a series of small booklets concerning the writings of a Bulgarian philosopher and musician by the name of Beinsa Douno. The purpose of this was to introduce this philosopher and musician (also known as Peter Dunov) to the Scottish and British public. Beinsa Douno had founded what is known as *Paneurythmy*, a form of Sacred Dance.

Before his death in 1944 Beinsa Douno had stated his conviction that, as we reach the New Millennium and then go beyond it, "the door to Heaven would then be opened", and it would be opened by means of Music. Again we see from philosophical writings that the importance of Music is paramount.

By the end of the nineteenth century Musical Theories of Expression and Composition were adopted as the means for the advancement of Architecture and Painting. As it happened, at the time it was Richard Wagner who was to influence the *avant-garde* more than any other composer.

Endell and Kandinsky were among those Artists for whom the apparent *universal* expressiveness of Music held out the possibility of there being an actual *abstract* visual Art. Its validity would be secured, *not* by reference to the appearances of the material or physical world but by supposedly basic formal principles on the one hand and the promptings of *inner necessity* on the other (12).

In 1917 there was the formation of *De Stijl* group in Holland, the members of which were dedicated to the synthesis of Art, Design and Architecture. The group was led by Theo van Doesburg.

As *De Stijl* saw it there was an Old and a New Consciousness of Time. The Old Consciousness was connected with the *individual* whereas the New was concerned with the *universal*. They believed that the New Art was *destined* to bring forward what the New Consciousness of Time contains, which is a balance between the individual and the universal (13). Traditions, dogmas and *the domination of the individual* were all opposed to this realisation.

Alexander Blok stated in *The Spirit of Music* when referring to the Russian Revolution, that it (the Revolution) was not just a fundamental change in all our outward life but something much more. It was the birth of a new kind of man the like of whom had never been seen on Earth before.

As Blok saw it, every movement had its birth in *The Spirit of Music* and then it degenerated. The Human Culture of the future would be nourished by what was akin to those musical and will-stressed floods and forces to which Richard Wagner had especially given expression. He stated further,

I sum up and draw the conclusion that there can be no shadow of doubt as to the final outcome of the struggle and that a new movement, born out of the spirit of music, has taken the place of the old human civilisation. So far it still resembles a runaway stream which carries with it the debris of civilisation. But already in this movement a metamorphosis out of which the new personality is to emerge is taking shape: not the ethical, political or humanist being but, in the words of Wagner, the creative being, the artistic person, who alone will be capable of living life in the epoch of storms and whirlwinds into which Mankind has unwittingly jettisoned itself (14).

Piet Mondrian (15), the Dutch abstract painter, had dedicated himself to "the elimination of all *non-essential* elements" in his work. His ultimate goal was "the expression of pure reality".

Mondrian believed in the transforming power of Art. He wanted to secure the *absolute autonomy* of the work of Art with respect to the perception *of* the object in the physical world. Liberated from its dependence upon Nature, the work of Art was free to acquire its own essence.

Mondrian reasoned that *representational* Art was not capable of generating a *universal reality* because it only reveals the *superficial appearance* of things, that is, it merely *describes.* Mondrian dedicated his work and his writings to 'the man of the future'. Works of Art, indeed, were meant to act as 'doors of perception'. They had to contribute to the personal enrichment of the viewer.

Mondrian believed that this New Spirit brought to a conclusion an Epoch during which the Artist painted only to *describe* nature whereas now a New Beauty was being created. This was indispensable to the Artist who is actually *creating his own image* in equivalent opposition to Nature.

Art would eventually disappear as life gains increasingly more beauty. Art was very important as it could prove in a *physical* manner, independent of our individual conceptions, the laws which can determine the development of a truly Human life.

By giving shape to the *Icons* of future Society, creative artists, acting as *visionaries,* can suggest the way by which a fuller life can be attained; according to this view, the artist is a kind of *initiate* capable of sensing the invisible and presenting it in a more *accessible* form.

In 1917 Mondrian stated:

Until today, the various ages of Civilisation had come into existence by the intermediary of a single individual (positioned above and on the margin of the community at large) who was able to quicken in the masses a sense of the universal. Initiates, saints and gods have brought to the people, as if from outside, the *recognition* of the universal, and with it an understanding of stylistic purity (16).

Mondrian developed a program which conceived the work of Art as a vehicle for expressing the force and harmony of the Universe by exclusively *physical* means.

III

The reason why the British Empire will be resurrected is because it is *the will of God* that it should happen. The British Empire was not built on force; indeed, *more* than any other Empire *of the time*, it was built on tillage and the desire to stimulate trade. As stated earlier, the British Empire was very liberal for the time; because of this God *favours* the British to lay the foundations for a New Global Order which will last 'until times indefinite'.

One of the pre-requisites for entering the future Kingdom is compassion. This is something the importance of which was recognised by Richard Wagner.

In his *Crowning Achievement*, the Opera known as *Parsifal*, Wagner brings this to our notice:

> The foundation of ethics is not rationality but compassion, and that it is through compassion, not through cleverness, that the deepest understanding of things is to be attained; this is the case because in the ultimate recesses of our being all living creatures are one and, therefore, the sufferings of each are the sufferings of all (17).

Wagner was to realise that the *intuitive* or *impulsive* part of his nature was the *most important*; his success was due to going beyond intellectual understanding to realising the importance of *feeling*.

We see this from something Wagner stated to an associate named Rockel, in a letter dated 23 August 1856:

> Would you suppose it possible for an artist to be helped to a clear understanding of his own work by an intelligence other than his own? As to this, I am in a position to speak as on this very point I have had the strangest experiences. Seldom has there taken place in the soul of one and the same man so profound a division and estrangement between the intuitive or impulsive part of his nature and his consciously or reasonably held ideas. For I must confess to having arrived at a clear understanding of my own works of art through the help of another, who has provided me with the reasoned conceptions corresponding to my *intuitive* principles.
>
> The period during which I have worked in obedience *to my intuitions* dates from *The Flying Dutchman*. *Tannhauser* and *Lohengrin* followed and, if there is any expression of an underlying poetic motive in these works it is to be sought in the sublime tragedy of renunciation, the negation of the will, where here appears as necessary and inevitable, and alone capable of working redemption. It was this deep underlying idea that gave to my poetry and my music that peculiar consecration, without which they would not have had that power to move profoundly which they have. Now the strange thing is that in all the conceptions at which I had arrived in the course of my struggles to understand the world with my conscious reason, I was working *in direct opposition to the intuitive ideas* expressed in these works. Whilst as an artist I *felt*, and with such convincing certainty that all my creations took their colour from my feelings, as a philosopher I sought to discover a *totally opposed* interpretation of the world: and this interpretation once discovered, I obstinately held to it, though to my own surprise I found that it had invariably to go to the wall when confronted by my *spontaneous* and purely objective *artistic intuitions*. I made my most remarkable discovery in this respect with my *Nibelung*

Drama. It had taken form at a time when, with my ideas, I had built up an optimistic world, on Hellenic principles; believing that in order to realise such a world it was only necessary for men to wish it. *I ingeniously set aside the problem why they did not wish it.* I remember it was with this definite purpose that I conceived the possibility of *Siegfried*, with the intention of representing an existence free from pain. But I meant in the presentment of the whole *Nibelung Drama* to express my meaning even more clearly, by showing how from the first wrongdoing a whole world of injustice arose, and consequently fell to pieces in order to teach us the lesson that we must recognise injustice and tear it up by the roots, and raise in its stead a righteous world. I was scarcely aware that in the working out, nay, in the first elaboration of my scheme, I was being *consciously guided* by a wholly different, infinitely more *profound intuition*, and that instead of conceiving a phase in the development of the world I had grasped the very essence and meaning of the world itself, in all its possible phases, and had realised its nothingness; the consequence of which was, that as I was true to my living intuition and *not* to my abstract ideas in my completed work, something quite different saw the light from what I had originally intended. But I remember once, towards the end, I decided to bring out my original purpose, cost what it might, namely, in Brunnhilde's final and somewhat artificially coloured invocation to those around her, in which, having pointed out the evils of possession, she declares that in love alone is blessedness to be found without, unfortunately, making quite clear what the nature of that love is, which in the development of *The Myth*, we find playing the part of a destructive genius. To this extent I was led astray in this one passage by the interposition of my intellectual intention. Strangely enough, I was always in despair over this said passage and it required the complete subversion of my intellectual conceptions, brought about by Schopenhauer, to discover to me the reason of my dissatisfaction, and to supply me with the only adequate keystone to my poem in keeping with the whole idea of the *Drama*, which consists in a simple and sincere recognition of the true relation of things, and the *complete abstinence* from the attempt to preach any *particular doctrine* (18).

Those who pass through the tribulation which will befall us and on into the *predestined* Kingdom of God will not be those who are expert in *Doctrinal* matters. They will be those whose lives are characterised by compassion.

The elect of God (19) will have no need to intellectualise their faith because their *intuition,* their *inclination* and their *predisposition* will permit them to recognise the Great Shepherd.

We will not need to go looking for this Person for this Person will come *to us,* as has been promised. It is for this reason that the New Testament tells us that:

> Every eye will see him and every knee shall bow and every tongue confess Him Lord, to the glory of God, the Father (20).

This person, whether we refer to Him as Krishna, as Hermes Trismegistus or as Ion, the Son of Apollo, will reveal the will of God to us by means of the language of God, which is *Music.*

Wars will take place, millions may be wiped out and hopelessness will be difficult to dislodge and still the Old Age will not end. The New Age will not begin until the preparation has been completed and *then* it will happen. Then there will be the dawning of the New Age. A New Day will dawn. It will begin when, all over the planet, people will be witness to *The Summoning of Apollo.*

We will be guided into the future by Music, the Ultimate Revelation of Reality; this will be possible because Apollo, or Krishna, or Ion, the Son of Apollo will have been revealed to us.

Those who receive guidance from this Apollo, this Krishna, will enter the Kingdom; after this the Divine Humanity will appear. This will herald the arrival of the Biblical Angels who will assimilate the Human Race into their Greater Life, which is also the Life of God.

The Human Race will be subsumed by this Greater Life of God; what the Ultimate Ancestor requires is a Collective Consciousness which can fully reflect the glory of the Godhead. In so doing It will have to be able to live on an endless basis by being an expression of the Divine Predisposition to *be* God.

This Collective Consciousness must be able to express the Absoluteness of God in terms of Consciousness. Because everything emanates from the Greater Life, this Greater Life will continue on an endless basis creating Its Own Reality for the consideration of the Divine Self.

NOTES

(1) James VI, King of Scots, left Edinburgh on the 5 March 1603. In the Ancient World the 5 March was the day dedicated to Isis, the principal Egyptian goddess.

It is interesting to note that in his book, *Redcoats and Rebels*, which was published in 2006 by *The Folio Society*, Christopher Hibbert mentions (on page 20) that:

> For years, until 4 July became a day of national celebration instead, 5 March was annually commemorated in Boston as a day worthy of the most solemn remembrance.

The quatercentenary of the death of Elizabeth I was on the 24 March 2003; there was a simultaneous accession of the new James I, or *the Union of the Crowns*, which accompanied it.

There is a point to consider here:

> Dates are not always when they seem to be. Until 1752 the dating of the years in England was not as we understand it today. New Year's Day was on the 25th of March. So in 1603 it was still the rule to date the year *not* from the 1st of January, but from Lady Day: the 25th of March. Therefore, in Elizabethan dating, January, February and most of March would still be in what we think of as the *previous* year. We would say that Elizabeth I died on the 24th of March 1603, whereas Tudor dating would have it as the 24th March, the final day of 1602.

See Christopher Lee, *1603*. First published in 2003 by REVIEW. An imprint of Headline Book Publishing. From the author's note, page x.

(2) The author (John Houston) cannot remember exactly what he heard or even when he heard it but it happened during an interview on the BBC World Service. A man being interviewed said that "if the United States of America and the United Kingdom step out of line with the United Nations in connection with the Iraqi situation then, whether we like it

or not, that will be *the end* of multi-lateral attempts to establish a global order".

(3) *The Book of Daniel*, chapter 2.44.

(4) The Asteroid which crashed into the Yucatan Peninsula 65 million years ago was, itself, probably part of the outcome of a head-on collision between two gigantic space rocks around 160 million years ago.

The two gigantic Asteroids were ripped apart as they collided at the speed of 3 kms per second, spawning thousands of smaller Asteroids, known collectively as *The Baptistina Family*.

(5) Michael Boulter, *Extinction; Evolution and the End of Man*. Published by *Fourth Estate*, which is a division of Harper/Collins in 2002, page 39.

(6) as (5) above. See page 47.

(7) as (5) above. See page 182.

(8) John Burnet, *Greek Philosophy*. Published by *The MacMillan Press*, London, 1981 edition, page 98.

(9) As we pass through the Tribulation and on into *The New Age*, it is for God to *provide* guidance for us.

As a young boy at Sunday school I remember clearly being told by the Church of Scotland minister that when the Children of Israel, who had been enslaved in Egypt for four centuries, left to journey on towards the Promised Land they had *no* need to discover the direction they should follow. They were *guided* by a Pillar of Cloud by day and by a Pillar of Fire by night.

Moses led the others. When either Pillar moved so did Moses and *only* in the direction indicated by the Pillar.

The Rulers to emerge to guide us through to the New Age will, themselves, have to be obeyed as the Biblical Moses, himself, is portrayed as being *entitled*.

When the author (John Houston) left the Scottish Green Party in 1992 while a member of its National Council, it was because I had become convinced that the problems with which the Human Race will have to deal would not be dealt with in any satisfactory manner *without Dictatorship.*

The Ruling Elite to come will operate as *Benign Dictators*; at the same time they will be aware that they cannot guide and motivate people without *Consent*, thus the term Benign Dictatorship.

(10) *The Book of Leviticus*, chapter 22.10-11. See also *The Book of Deuteronomy*, chapter 21.10-14.

(11) *The Letter of Paul to Philemon*, verses 10-17.

(12) Charles Harrison & Paul Wood, *Art in Theory 1900-2000. An Anthology of Changing Ideas*. New Edition. Published by Blackwell in 2002. From *The Introduction*, page 13.

(13) as (12) above. See page 281.

Others involved were Gerrit Rietveld and J.J.P. Oud, both of whom were Architect-Designers and the painters Georges Vantongerloo and Piet Mondrian.

(14) as (12) above. See page 263.

(15) Piet Mondrian lived from 1872 until 1944. He had become known as such upon his arrival in Paris in 1912. Prior to this he had been Pieter Cornelius Mondrian. In 1892 he had enrolled at *The Academy of Fine Arts* in Amsterdam; at this time he encountered *esotericism*, most notably through an association with *The Theosophical Society*. This led to his estrangement from Calvinism.

(16) Cameo/Abrams, *Mondrian*. Published by Harry N. Abrams Inc., New York. See page 22.

(17) Bryan Magee, *Wagner and Philosophy*. Published by Allen Lane in 2000. The Penguin Press. From the chapter, *Crowning Achievement*, which relates to the Opera *Parsifal*. See page 273.

(18) as (17) above. From the chapter, *Wagner Re-evaluates His Values*. See page 187.

(19) as (17) above. From the chapter *Wagner and Nietzsche*, and on page 300 we read:

> By this time Nietzsche had long thought of himself and Wagner as sharing 'the inmost community of our endeavours and thoughts under the *one* flag' (letter dated 12 December 1870). With the publication of *The Birth of Tragedy* he declared: "I have made an alliance with Wagner. You cannot imagine how close we are now, and how our plans coincide" (letter 28 January 1872). Until about 1876, when he was thirty-two, he dreamt of founding some sort of community of the elect which was to include both circles of their acquaintanceship, who tended naturally to centre on different age groups. As the translator of his letters, Christopher Middleton, has said: "It was to be a system of friends, with a spiritual centre in Bayreuth, that should regenerate and transform German society, in the names of Schopenhauer and Wagner."

(20) *The Epistle of Paul to the Philippians*, chapter 2.9-10.

8: The Multi-Faceted Tradition

I

When George Gemistos Plethon appeared on the scene in Florence in 1439, he was to have a profound influence on those around him. For Plethon there were certain beliefs or truths which he considered to be fundamental.

For Plethon, the Western Philosophical Tradition had come down to those at *The Council of Florence* in 1439 from a source which went back to Zoroaster (1), the greatest of the Magi. In the final analysis, the source of Human Civilisation was *not* Ancient Egypt, but earlier in Europe, and even that was *not* the beginning for, as a Platonist, he would have known that Plato had mentioned Atlantis (2).

The world was not yet ready to receive his counsel and, accordingly, he was to become associated with and *considerably influence* a movement which sought to see Jesus of Nazareth and the prophet Muhammed *replaced* by Hermes Trismegistus. Later on the prophet, Giovanni Mercurio da Correggio, called for the *Hermetic Reformation* of Christianity and Islam.

Plethon had wanted to see Plato revered as the greatest philosopher of all; Plethon regarded Zoroaster and his disciples to be the *first* Guardians of Truth having lived at a time much earlier than either Moses or Hermes Trismegistus; Plethon claimed that Orpheus was *the first* Guardian of Hellenic

(Greek) Theology, which was cultivated in more remote times by *The Kouretes*, from Crete; Plethon claimed that Pythagoras, *the Ionian*, had introduced the Teachings of Zoroaster to the Greeks and from them to Plato.

In spite of what Plethon had to say it was *The Corpus Hermeticum*, allegedly of *Egyptian origins*, which made its reappearance after a millennium. This was so because of the person of Hermes Trismegistus, *The Messenger of the gods*, with whom the Egyptians had become familiar and whom they recognised as synonymous with Thoth of the ibis beak, the Great Law-Giver and Servant of God.

Thoth and Hermes were both regarded as being *Egyptian in origin*; indeed they were *both* recognised as being *synonymous* with the Biblical Moses, also a Law-Giver.

The Mythology of the known world tended to look back to Ancient Egypt. Why should there have been such a fascination with Egypt? It had everything to do with belief in a Suprahistorical Person who appears in the great Mythologies of the Ancient World. In the Popular Mythology of the time, which existed at street level, *nothing and no one* went further back in time than the Pharaohs of Egypt. Knowing more required Initiation.

> Ancient Egyptians ascribed to Thoth Theological, Liturgical and Technical Writings copied in the House of Life, that is, the Scriptorium of a Temple. Consequently, as early as the third or second century BC until the third century AD, there appeared Greek Writings on Astrology and Alchemy (3) as well as Magical Recipes and Philosophical Treatises *said* to have been translated from the Egyptian language and authored by Hermes Trismegistus.
>
> Recent research on Hermetic Religion has resolved several problems, and the Coptic Hermetic texts from Nag Hammadi have shed light on these issues. First with regard to the matter of Egyptian origins, we should note that Roman Egypt, where the philosophical Hermetica were written, is very different from Pharaonic Egypt. Roman Egypt displays an intellectual and religious syncretism that combines with the Egyptian cultural core several successive strata, from the Iranian conquest of Cambyses (4) up to the Hellenic and Roman periods. However, according to *Hermetic dogma*, Egypt, as the *Mother* of Human Civilisation, cannot possibly have received any foreign influence.

On the contrary, she has always been the Teacher of other nations.

As the Priest of Sais explains to Solon, the culture of the world has been periodically swallowed up by various cataclysms, except in Egypt, which has always been protected by the Nile. Therefore, the wise of other nations necessarily depend upon Egypt.

The truths found in Moses' *Genesis* and Plato's *Timaeus* can be traced back to the antediluvian writings of Hermes-Thoth. As a result, when Hermetic writers seemingly borrow ideas from Jewish or Greek sources, they are simply returning to Egypt her own heritage, stolen by foreigners.

Second, most scholars currently agree that Hermetism is *not* a philosophical system but a spiritual *way*. Consequently, despite apparent contradictions that we may note in the texts, we should not contrast Gnostic with non-Gnostic Hermetic Writings. In fact, non-Gnostic Hermetic Writings constitute the beginnings of the quest for God: those searching for the Divine first have to become aware of his invisible presence through his visible creatures.

Third, the discovery of the Coptic Hermetica confirms that Hermetic Religion, far from being a mere literary phenomenon, was an actual religious movement with a deep social impact, based on congregations quite similar to Gnostic communities. The Hermetic worshippers accepted popular Religion and admired the Traditional Cults of Egypt, which they called "the Holy Land of their Ancestors", a country "more godly than any other country", the "dwelling place of the gods" and "the School of Religion" (5).

There was no mention of UR III; that Civilisation which was well and truly ended around 3000 BC. For those at *The Council of Florence*, UR III could never be anything more than the stuff of legend, if they had heard of UR III at all (6). In general, they would not have been aware *how* the smouldering embers of UR III gave rise to Civilisation in Egypt, as well as in India. They would not have known *how* Civilisation had also taken hold in the land between the Tigris and the Euphrates. That Knowledge was kept *secret* and only available to *Initiates*.

In Mesopotamian literature we read of Enki, the god of Wisdom, who was "overpowering in his majesty". Enki stated:

My Father
The King of the Universe
Brought me into Existence
In the Universe.

My Ancestor
The King of all the Lands
Gathered together all the me's
And placed the me's
In my hand.

I am 'the Great Storm'
Who goes forth
Out of 'the Great below'
I am the Lord of the Land.

I am 'the Big Brother'
Of the gods.
I am he who brings
Full prosperity.

I am the record keeper
Of Heaven and Earth.
I am the ear and mind
Of all the Lands.

I am He who directs Justice
With King An.
I am He who decrees the Fates
With Enlil
In 'the Mountain of Wisdom'.

The influence of Ancient Egypt cannot be accurately measured but it is immense and people were in awe of Egypt, whose neighbours saw it as a land "of gold as plentiful as dust" which was too powerful to attack.

For the Greeks, Egypt was the home of an unimaginably ancient language and mysterious religious Traditions *rumoured* to possess Secret Knowledge which pertained to the gods. For the Romans, Egypt was the granary which fed the Empire but which profoundly fascinated all Romans.

It would be centuries before Ancient Egypt was rediscovered and Archaeologists were to piece together the astonishing story of Ancient Egypt. People would learn that by the Third Dynasty (7) there was a new phase in Egyptian history for the Rulers were in absolute control of the country and possessed awesome power.

The earlier Kings emphasised Horus and Seth as *the Royal gods*. Although these gods were not abandoned entirely, the Third Dynasty Kings were *themselves* to be worshipped as the direct descendants of Ra, the Sun god.

Ra, they claimed, would appear *in Human form* to impregnate an earthly mother; in theory this could be any woman but, in practice, the King would announce that Ra, *disguised as the King*, in seeking couplement with the Queen had made her pregnant and her son, when born, would in fact be a child of the Sun god.

The Mythology did not end there for the Divinity of the baby would have to be confirmed. This was undertaken by Thoth of the ibis beak, *The Messenger of the gods*, who, in appearing to the Queen, would inform her of her good fortune.

II

We are informed that up until the time of Pythagoras (8), *The Milesian Tradition* was dominant within the Western Philosophical Tradition. With the Fall of Miletos in 494 BC the Milesian School of Philosophy *allegedly* came to an end. The philosophy of Anaximines continued to be taught in Ionian cities; furthermore, those Teachings pertaining to Orpheus were beginning to spread in every direction.

The Old and New Testaments have both been handed down to us in the form of *The Myth of Orpheus and Eurydice*, both of whom had lived on a world far higher than this one is at present. Eurydice was bitten by a serpent and *died*; in consequence, she came *here*. Orpheus followed intent upon redeeming her by means of his Music (9).

Then Pythagoras came on the scene. As an Ionian he would have revered Apollo above all the other gods and here we should remember that George Gemistos Plethon claimed that Pythagoras had introduced the philosophy of Zoroaster to the Greeks. The point in question is this: are the Zoroastrian Traditions mentioned by Plethon *the same* as those Traditions referring to Ion, the Son of Apollo?

In *The Euthydemus* of Plato we read of a conversation of which Socrates is informing us:

> What a miserable man you must be then, he said; you are not an Athenian at all if you have no ancestral gods or temples, or any other mark of gentility.
>
> Nay, Dionysodorus, I said, do not be rough; good words, if you please; in the way of religion I have altars and temples, domestic and ancestral, and all that other Athenians have.
>
> And have not other Athenians, he said, an ancestral Zeus?
>
> That name, I said, is not to be found among the Ionians, whether colonists or citizens of Athens; *an ancestral Apollo there is, who is the father of Ion*, and a family Zeus, and a Zeus guardian of the phratry, and an Athene guardian of the phratry. But the name of ancestral Zeus is unknown to us (10).

The importance of understanding the significance of Pythagoras and those Traditions which may be identified with him is that to a great extent those Traditions which were dear to him were also held in the highest esteem within Gaeldom, or the Ancient Scots. Here we can recall those Traditions which claim that Pythagoras was instructed by Druids.

We must recognise that the Western Philosophical Tradition had evolved considerably from the time of Thales; and Pythagoras was of considerable importance. He would reveal the cause of eclipses, for example, indeed much more than that. He would have worshipped Apollo and would have been familiar with those Traditions pertaining to Ion, the Son of Apollo, which were prominent within Gaeldom.

Gaeldom, those Ancient Scots whose language was Gaidhlig, existed long before Pythagoras was alive; indeed Gaeldom goes much further back than

Zoroaster. The Old Gaidhlig existed prior to 2000 BC, so Gaeldom has had a long and very illustrious journey through Space and Time (11).

When the Ancient Scots forsook Ireland to found the Kingdom of Dal Riada in what would become known as Scotland, the location which became their spiritual focus was a small island to be known as *Iona*, where Saint Columba founded his monastery in 563 AD, with Iona being named in honour of *Ion*, the Son of Apollo.

Centuries later, when Marsilio Ficino was translating texts for Cosimo de' Medici he was operating against a background of great respect for Ancient Egypt. He would have become aware of Hermes Trismegistus and Thoth of the ibis beak, both of whom were deemed to be *synonymous* with the Biblical Moses, with whom there was an indelible Egyptian connection.

Undermining Moses was inadvisable. It could lead to Marsilio Ficino's motives being misconstrued.

The Medici were *not* in the position to unconditionally accept the outlook of Plethon. Were they to do that then they would have found themselves in the unfortunate position of *undermining the authority* of the Bible. The Medici would have known that the world was not yet ready for this and it is for this reason that they were prepared to accept the *equality* of the Biblical Revelation with *The Corpus Hermeticum*. This would have suited their purpose.

Giovanni Mercurio da Correggio had sought to reinforce the belief that there was an *absolute equality* between the Hermetic Tradition and the Christian Revelation as found in the Bible. Obviously this suited his purpose, seeing that he considered himself to be Christ reincarnate.

At the time of the Renaissance the Medici family had befriended Plethon just as they would do with Marsilio Ficino who, it has been claimed, basked in fine philosophical fellowship whilst imitating Orpheus (12).

Plethon came to *The Council of Florence* with a message for the entire world which at the time had been beguiled by the Royal Lie, as propagated by the Vatican. We would learn from his experience the Truth that Moses Maimonides (13), the great Jewish philosopher, had stated:

> It is impossible to go from one particular state or condition to an opposite state or condition *without* the necessity of an *interim* stage.

The Human Race could not go from indoctrination by the Royal Lie *to* the Truth of the message pertaining to the Kingdom of God *without* this Interim Stage.

By the same token it would not have been possible, at the time of the Reformation, for the Scots to go from Catholicism (the Royal Lie) to those *Mysteries* pertaining to Ion, the Son of Apollo, without the interim stage which is known to us as Protestantism.

People who come from a Protestant background have a tendency to underestimate the power and influence that *The Cult of Mary*, the Virgin goddess, exerted over Medieval Christianity.

Medieval Christianity was dominated by Mary, "the Mother of God", a state of affairs with which the Protestant Reformers had to deal. They were to discover that the Religion of Mary was so deeply ingrained.

Queen Elizabeth, in guiding England through the troubled Reformation times, out of *necessity* had to go to the extent of becoming a *visible representation* of the Virgin goddess.

Queen Elizabeth, having *adopted* the identity of the Virgin Mary offered herself as a *substitute* for the Virgin Queen. This involved an outward show of remaining unmarried and, therefore, a *Virgin*, in spite of her *alleged* affair which *allegedly* produced two sons.

The first British colony, established in *Virginia* in 1607, was named in honour of the Virgin Queen of England who had come to replace the Catholic Mary.

This also gives us an insight as to why it was not until 1752 that the dating of the year became that to which we are accustomed today. In 1752, New Year's Day became the first day of January; prior to this New Year's Day was the twenty-fifth day of March, known also as Lady Day, the first day of the year being dedicated to *Our Lady*, the Virgin goddess, the Queen of the Universe and Great Provider for her children.

There will come a time when the need for that interim stage will be no more; the Truth will have been revealed to the Human Race. Those capable of receiving the Truth will be initiated into *The Mysteries*. It will become known that, by means of the Human Race, the Ultimate Ancestor will be able to manifest Itself as a Collective Consciousness. Humanity exists as the provision of the Divine Identity.

Accordingly, philosophers of the future will recognise the importance of Zoroaster and his philosophy which looked to Apollo and then to Ion, the Son of Apollo, as a noble School of Philosophy (14).

NOTES

(1) Zoroaster (or Zarathustra) lived from around 630 BC until 553 BC. The religious reformer is believed to have been born somewhere near modern Tehran. He claimed to have seen a vision of *Ahura Mazda*, the Wise Lord, resulting in *Ahura Mazda* becoming central to the reformed Religion of Iran, which had formerly been polytheistic.

Zoroaster believed *Ahura Mazda* was the only God *worthy* of worship, recognised by Zoroaster as being characterised by Justice, Truth, Wholeness and Immortality. At a future date it was anticipated that a Righteous Kingdom would appear on Earth.

(2) Plato mentioned Atlantis in *The Timaeus* and in *The Critias*.

(3) The word *Alchemy* is believed to be of Arabic origin. A popular explanation is that it meant 'the Art of the Land of Khem', with Khem being the name the Arabs gave to Egypt; it was from Egypt that they acquired their knowledge of this strange Science, which they later transmitted to the West.

On the other hand, it is possible that the word is derived from the Greek *chymia*, which denotes the Art of melting and alloying metals.

(4) In 550 BC, Cambyses I, King of Persia died and was succeeded by his son Cyrus II. This Cyrus the Great, which is how Cyrus II would be remembered, created a new Persian Empire uniting the Medes, the Persians and other peoples. This is how Persia became the world's first *superpower*.

(5) *The Gnostic Gospels*, edited by Marvin Meyer. *Incorporating The Sacred Writings of the Nag Hammadi Library, The Berlin Gnostic Codex and Codex Tchaos.* Published by *The Folio Society*, London in 2008. From the chapter, *Hermetic Religion*. See page 689.

(6) The purpose of *Ibis Initiation Time* is *not* history as such but to render available to others the philosophy of John Houston, the Scots philosopher and mystic.

When UR III is mentioned this is done in recognition of the fact that, around 3000 BC, forces conspired to see a whole new Epoque in the growth of Human Culture.

By 3000 BC, in Egypt, King Menes founds the first of Egypt's historical dynasties; Egyptians develop copper mines in Sinai; the cuneiform script becomes formalised among the Sumerians; the potter's wheel appears in China; cotton fabric is being woven in the Indus Valley.

(7) The Third Dynasty of Ancient Egypt begins in 2630 BC when Djoser (the Most Sacred One) becomes King. During the reign of Djoser the first Pyramid is built under the direction of Imhotep, the first Architect known to History.

In 2575 BC, the accession of Snefru (the Bringer of Beauty) to the throne marks the beginning of the Old Kingdom Period. Snefru is commemorated in the two Pyramids of Dahshur at Memphis.

(8) Pythagoras was one of the most mysterious and influential figures in Greek intellectual history; the name of Pythagoras is connected with two parallel Traditions.

He was famous for the Geometric Theorem that still bears his name; even more significant for Pythagorean Thought is the discovery of Musical Consonances. It was said that Pythagoras understood 'the Music of the Spheres' which, apparently, *only* Pythagoras could hear.

Plato was deeply influenced by the Pythagorean Traditions, especially Pythagoras' conception of the soul *transcending* the body as well as Pythagoras' Mathematical Interpretation of Nature.

(9) According to Orpheus the body is a tomb in which the soul is kept in custody, life after life until liberation is reached. Orpheus was also convinced that as far as common parlance is concerned, the words *life* and *death* were improperly used. What we refer to as *life* is actually *death* with the body a tomb for the soul.

(10) *The Dialogues of Plato*. Translated by J. Harward. Published by *The Encyclopaedia Britannica, Inc.*, Chicago in 1996. See Page 82.

(11) The origins of Gaeldom are ancient and now lost in the mists of Antiquity. As far as Gaeldom's language (Gaidhlig) is concerned, it too

is very ancient; the *Old* Gaidhlig is often depicted as existing prior to 2000 BC.

Let us put this date of 2000 BC into perspective; it is but a few decades after King Mentuhotep's restoration of centralised government in Egypt marks the beginning of the Middle Kingdom; construction of the main stage of the Stonehenge Megalithic Stone Circle is completed in what is now England; there is the emergence of the Minoan Palace Civilisation on the isle of Crete; the new power of Babylon is developing decimal notation; written in Sumerian cuneiform, the world's first written Myth, *The Epic of Gilgamesh*, appears, mentioning a Great Flood from which Humanity is rescued by the building of an Ark.

(12) Howard Hubbard, *Michelangelo*. With *An Introduction* by Michael Levey. Published by *The Folio Society*, London in 2007. See page 6.

The glory of Florence in the Quattrocento was, at least in retrospect, her Art. The artists in a sense served two masters, religious institutions and the State. But all patronage, ultimately, came from individuals, whether for a painted family chapel or a Neoplatonic allegory of Spring.

Lorenzo himself was not a great patron (he was not a Prince and had no real court) but he had a splendid collection of antiquities and an even more impressive collection of intellectuals grouped around the philosopher Marsilio Ficino.

Ficino sought to reconcile antique Platonic ideas, especially those later, mystical doctrines associated with Plotinus, and Christian belief. This syncretism was not so hard a task as it sounds and the men around Lorenzo must often have been buoyed by a sense of coming ever closer to the philosophical secrets at the core of Man's existence.

Ficino also liked to play the part of a modern Orpheus, *entertaining the Medici with his lyre*; Lorenzo himself wrote poetry and acted in triumphal pageants.

It was into this hedonistic humanistic world that the young Michelangelo was thrust when he was about fifteen years of age. All his life he kept a Neoplatonic vocabulary, and his poetry written years later, may sometimes reflect the diction of the Medici circle.

But it was the literal humanism of these men, the new importance they gave to Man himself, that most influenced Michelangelo and that differentiates him from earlier artists.

(13) Moses Maimonides (originally Moses ben Maimon), the great Jewish philosopher, was born in Cordoba, Spain in 1135 AD. He studied Medicine and Aristotelian philosophy and then in 1165, he moved to Egypt, settling in Cairo where he became physician to Saladin, the head of the Jewish community.

Maimonides was the foremost figure of Medieval Judaism; his greatest work, *The Guide to the Perplexed*, written in 1190, argued for the reconciliation of Greek philosophy with Judaism. He died in 1204.

(14) Apollo was pre-eminently the god of the Greeks, their central conception of Him as being the god of Light. Later poets recognised him as the Sun god, although Homer recognised Helios and Apollo as two *distinct* Divinities.

Corresponding to the external light of the world the Greeks recognised the internal Light of the Mind, known as *noumenal* Light.

His origins are obscure and there is a school of thought which states that he was a purely Doric Divinity whose first Temples were at Tempe and Delphi. His worship spread into Attica and Crete and from there to wherever the Ionians settled.

Apollo is represented as being in the prime of youth and of being elegantly and finely-proportioned with a countenance of perfect beauty. His instrument was the four-stringed lyre.

In *The Cratylus* of Plato, we read of Socrates referring to Apollo. Socrates says, "and is not Apollo the purifier, and the washer and the absolver from all impurities?"

9: The Legacy of Gaeldom

I

From the Fall of Atlantis those *Mysteries of Atlantis* would have been taken to the four corners of the Earth. This is why the Ancient Mythologies greatly concur. They stem from a common source, a source which would have been a reflection of the world view of those *Fragments* who were master mariners and supreme educators.

The common source from which they emanated was that Civilisation which ended around 3000 BC in Europe. This would, itself, have been a gathering ground for the various Traditions pertaining to the Origin and Destiny of the Human Race, Traditions which would have existed from the earliest of times (1).

Thereafter, according to legend, they were to sow the seeds of Dynastic greatness in Egypt. From what had been an *oral* Tradition of the Gaidhlig bards of the Scottish Highlands, mention is made of this.

One bard, Alexander MacDonald, in a piece of bardachd (poetry) entitled *The Resurrection of the Ancient Scottish Language* (2), states that there was an intimate connection between the Ancient Scots and the Pharaohs of Egypt. Alexander MacDonald, furthermore, *seems* to be of the opinion that Gaidhlig was the language spoken in the Garden of Eden.

The bard actually states that the Scots were descended from the Pharaohs of Egypt. These Ancient Scots would have had colonies all over the Mediterranean Sea and elsewhere. They were to influence all the other nations of the known world. Through their spiritual hierarchy, the Druids, they were to propagate an *Esoteric Tradition* which is as old as the Human Race.

The tenth century *Pictish Chronicle* attempted to integrate Scots and Picts into a single people by tracing them to both the Scythians and Scota, daughter of Pharaoh, explaining that they had white hair and were therefore called 'Albani'. The so-called 'Duan Albanach', composed during the reign of Malcolm Canmore (1058-93) opens with the Brutus origin legend, introduces the Picts, and soon replaces them with the triumphant Gaels. At the inauguration of King Alexander III in 1249, a Gaelic poet recited his genealogy back to Gaidheal Glas, son of Neolius King of Athens and his wife Scota, daughter of Pharaoh. These were not merely idle antiquarian ramblings, but mainstream contemporary political rhetoric.

In a letter to the Pope Boniface VIII, King Edward of England founded his title over Scotland's sovereignty on the Brutus legend (as given in *Historia Regum Britanniae* by Geoffrey of Monmouth c. 1135). The Scots, in reply, dismissed Edward's claims as 'ancient fables' and countered with the origin legend which paired Scota, daughter of the Pharaoh, with Gaidheal Glas, Ancestor of the Gaels. Their case was reviewed favourably in Rome and a plot summary of the legend opens the 'Declaration of Arbroath'.

Elements of the origin legend continued to recur in Gaelic political rhetoric, literature and poetry. When in 1701 the antiquarian Robert Wodrow sent a letter to John Maclean to get information from the learned John Beaton about Gathelus (the Latinised form of 'Gaidheal'), Maclean replied:

As for Gathelus, (Beaton) avers that indeed he is the progenitor of the *Scoti Antiqui*, who inhabited Ireland, whose genealogie he can shew (…). This, he says is neither fabulous or improbable, seeing there were records left by every generation to their posteritie, and these men were not (as ye suppose) unlearned, but great philosophers, Gathelus being the grandchild of

(Fenius Farsaid …) to Fergus MacRoiss, monarch of Ireland, and progenitor of the Kings of Great Britain of the Steuart race (3).

We have at our disposal certain ancient fragments from the historian Berossus, of which there was a general publication in 1876, which gives accounts from the Babylonian Tradition which maintained that Civilisation on Earth was founded by *amphibious* beings known as Oannes, or Musari or Annedoti, in Greek. These beings came from the system of *Sirius* (4).

These ancient fragments have come down to us by means of the custodianship of certain ancient historians, such as Apollodorus and Abydenus. It is maintained that these writings "contained a history of the heavens and the sea, of the birth of Mankind, also of those who had sovereign rule, and the actions achieved by them".

Fragments from the historian Berossus, who is reputed to have lived at the same time as Alexander the Great, have been preserved; they refer to the supremacy of the early Chaldean Kings, a supremacy which lasted until the time of the Great Deluge. Mention is made of this in R.E.O. Temple's book, *The Sirius Mystery*.

> This is the history which Berossus has transmitted to us. He tells us that the first king was Alorus of Babylon, a Chaldean; he reigned ten sari; and afterwards Alaparus, and Amelon who came from Pantibiblon: then Ammenon the Chaldean, in whose time appeared the Musarus Oannes the Annedotus from the Erythraean Sea. But Alexander Polyhistor anticipating the event, has said that he appeared in the first year; but Apollodorus says that it was after forty sari; Abydenus, however, makes the second Annedotus appear after twenty-six sari.

These are dynasties of Supermen, or so it would appear. While venerating the Wisdom of the Chaldeans we are informed that:

> Now a sarus is esteemed to be three thousand six hundred years; a neros is six hundred; and a sossus sixty.

From the beginnings of Civilisation until the time of the Great Deluge there was a lineage of ten kings and "the term of their reigns was a hundred and twenty sari". This is an exceptionally long period of time, over four hundred thousand years.

The rulers of the Human Race saw the end of their attempts to civilise Humanity; everything is viewed as being swept away. Thereafter:

> The gods introduced a variety of tongues among men who till
> that time had all spoken the same language.

We can only speculate where those whom we would later identify as the Ancient Scots were at this time. Gaeldom is ancient and those rulers identified as the early Chaldean kings would have had offspring who would be assimilated into other cultures which survived the legendary Deluge.

This would have happened in Europe in pre-history. Gaidhlig, like the other so-called Celtic languages, evolved alongside other languages with those languages most comparable to Gaidhlig being Russian on the one hand and Farsi (Persian) on the other.

II

As far as settlement in Great Britain and Ireland is concerned, there was a whole series of incursions prior to the one with which we are most concerned. This has to do with the arrival of the Milesians, with whom the Ancient Scots have a close connection, as is commonly held.

The leader of these master mariners was one known as Milesius, who had married Scota, the daughter of a Pharaoh of Egypt. These master mariners are said to have come to Ireland via Spain. These are the Scots and they gave Ireland its first name, which was *Scotia*.

So great had been their influence on Old Scotia, or Ireland, that when the King of Scots held court in Meath, he met with Druids, lesser kings and chieftains. In due course, with their supremacy *undermined*, the Scots were to commence their colonisation of Pictland which, in time, would become known as Scotland, or *Alba* in Gaidhlig, which was their language.

Saint Columba, also known as Colm Cille, which means 'the dove of the Church', had founded a monastery on Iona in 563 AD. He had gone there as that was the most suitable spot from which Ireland was not visible, not to mention that on the neighbouring and larger Isle of Mull there is a mountain (Beinn Mheadhanach) which bears a striking resemblance to a Pyramid.

Then at a meeting in Derry in 575 AD, Dal Riada, the Scots colony was declared to be independent of Ireland, in the presence of Saint Columba (5).

The Civilisation built by the Scots was remarkable. It would produce Clan Donald who would emerge as the Lords of the Isles. Modern research may suggest that Clan Donald (6) originated on the Isle of Man; their Civilisation was founded on a *Caste* system. Clan Donald were the Brahmins whilst the Morrisons (7) dealt with legal matters and the Beatons (8) with medical matters. They worshipped the Celtic Apollo, whom they revered as the Sun god (9).

With the passage of time that Lordship of the Isles, so proudly held by Clan Donald, was to disintegrate and then disappear. It was a stage in a process which would see the almost complete destruction of the Gaidhlig way of life, bequeathed to us by those Ancient Scots.

In many ways no more than a hazy memory remained. Almost all links with the Ancient Scots and their role in the establishing of Civilisation on Earth were to disappear, with one exception. This involved Knowledge in connection with a mythical Clan who had lived in the Scottish Highlands from *remote Antiquity*. Their allegiance would have been to Clan Donald and they were referred to as *AOS* (10).

Mention had been made of them but the word *AOS* was to fall into obsolescence. It appeared originally in a Gaidhlig Dictionary. There is a reference in Armstrong's *Scots Gaelic Dictionary* to the language spoken in mid-Perthshire in the Medieval Period. Even then it was described as a word *from remote Antiquity*, not even in use when Armstrong was compiling his Dictionary, which was sometime in the fifteenth or sixteenth century.

Armstrong was to define the word *AOS* as "The Sun. Fire. God. A *mythical* Clan who lived in mid-Perthshire". No mention is made of them elsewhere.

Why, one might ask, should Clan Donald, the Lords of the Isles, be linked to a mythical Clan *said* to have operated in mid-Perthshire? Why should mid-Perthshire have been so important? Why not some other part of the Highlands?

The answer may well be that mid-Perthshire was the place where the Kings of Scots were to be crowned (11). Perhaps this mythical Clan had a specific role to play in the Gaidhlig Civilisation. It would hardly be an outrage to suggest that they may have been an Esoteric Retinue for the Kings and

Queens of Scots. They would have provided advice on Druidic matters of which they were the Pre-eminent Masters.

These hazy recollections of both the ancientness and the greatness of Gaeldom remind us of the *possibility* of two things: the foundation of Human Civilisation did not come from Egypt as was *mistakenly* believed to have been the case, but from Europe, and from those who would emerge as the *Scots*; they did not die out but were always in the background as Human history unfolded.

They would have brought their belief systems with them as they eventually settled in the British Isles. The belief system which was dominant among them was to become beliefs involving Apollo or Ion, Son of Apollo (12).

They would have experienced cross-fertilisation at the time of the Scandinavian Empire, after which they would have become dominant throughout the time of the Lordship of the Isles which, in time, would go into decline. Then there was the subjection of the Royal Lie on the British Isles by means of the Norman Empire, whose task was to *impose* the Religion of Rome (*The Cult of Jesus Christ*) upon the British Isles.

The best was yet to come with the independence of the British Isles from European domination and the subsequent appearance of the British Empire to which the Scots contributed "a strain of incomparable value". No one did more to build and defend the British Empire than the Scots.

Now *the will of God* is that the British Empire be resurrected. The vision pursued by those Ancient Scots will have been realised; there will be the dawning of a Kingdom without end to unite the world, to lay the foundation for the next stage of Human evolution and *assimilation* into the Galactic Confederation.

NOTES

(1) With the demise of that Civilisation in Europe by around 3000 BC, Civilisation was to be ignited in Egypt, in India and in Mesopotamia. The language of that Civilisation, or its Ruling Elite, formed the basis for every modern European language with the exception of Basque, Finnish and Hungarian.

(2) The Gaidhlig name of the piece of bardachd is *Aiseiridh na Seann Canain Albannaich*.

(3)   Michael Newton, *Warriors of the Word. The World of the Scottish Highlanders*. With a foreword by Hugh Cheape. Published in 2009 by *Birlinn Limited*. From the chapter, *Identity and Ethnicity*, pages 56-57.

(4)   From Temple's book, *The Sirius Mystery*, page 250. *Fragments of Berossus from Alexander Polyhistor.*

In the first year, there made its appearance from a part of the Erythraean Sea which bordered upon Babylonia, an animal endowed with reason, who was called Oannes. According to the account of Apollodoras, the whole body of the animal was like that of a fish and had under a fish's head another head, and also feet below, similar to those of a man, subjoined to a fish's tail. His voice too, and language, was articulate and human; and a representation of him is preserved even to this day.

This Being in the daytime used to converse with men; but he took no food at that season, and he gave them an insight into letters and sciences, and every kind of art. He taught them to construct houses, to found temples, to compile laws, and explained to them the principles of geometrical knowledge. He made them distinguish the seeds of the Earth and showed them how to collect fruits. In short, he instructed them in everything which could tend to soften manners and *humanise* mankind.

(5)   The Gaidhlig for Derry is *Doire*. In Edward Dwelly's *Scots Gaelic to English Dictionary*, the word *Doire* means 'an isolated clump of trees, properly of oaks'. Parallels to the Greeks require no mention here but, nonetheless, here is a reminder; at the age of 42, Plato was then able to begin to teach in the *oak* grove known as *Akademos*.

(6)   On BBC2 Scotland there was an eight-part series on the Lordship of the Isles called *An Rioghachd nan Eilean* in Gaidhlig. *An Rioghachd nan Eilean* means 'The Lordship of the Isles'.

In one of the episodes the assertion was made that Clan Donald, referred to as *Na Domhnallaich*, actually originated on the Isle of Man. The Lords of the Isles and of Sleat, on the Isle of Skye, were known as the Clan *Mac Uisdein* or as the Clan *Mac Mhic Uisdein*, or as *the sons of Hugh*, or even *grandsons of Hugh*.

There is a Gaidhlig song known as *Mairi Uisdein* in which a woman called *Mairi Uisdein* falls asleep in front of the roaring fire and her legs become burnt and discoloured due to the excessive heat. In the song Mairi Uisdein is asked a question; what is your tartan, what is your tartan, what is your tartan, Mairi Uisdein? The discolouration of her legs obviously resembled tartan. Translations of Mairi Uisdein into English refer to Mairi Uisdein as *Mary Houston*.

MacDonald of Clanranald was *Mac Mhic Ailein*; MacDonald of Glenalladale was *Mac Iain Og*; MacDonald of Glencoe was *Mac Iain*; MacDonald of Glengarry was *Mac Mhic Alasdair*; MacDonald of Keppoch was *Mac Mhic Raonuill*.

(7) The Morrisons were known as *Na Moireasdanaich*. The surname Morrison, although usually *Moireasdan* in Gaidhlig, has another version used on the Isle of Lewis, which is *Mac Ghille Mhoire* or 'Son of the Servant of Mary, or Moire'. Obviously the Morrisons had a relationship with Moire, the Earth Mother who became Mary, the Mother of Jesus.

Dealing with legal matters they were also known as *Clann a' Bhreithimh*, the clan which *judges*.

(8) Beaton is the same name as Paton; in Gaidhlig the name is *Peudan*, with the name of the Clan being *Na Peudanaich*. They were also known as the *MacBheatha* doctors.

(9) Around 500 BC the Roman historian, Hecateus, visited Western Europe and he is the first person to use the term *Celt*. The name Hecateus denotes veneration for Hecate, a Roman goddess symbolic of *Sirius*.

Hecateus spoke of "Nyrax, a Celtic city" and of Massalia, now known as Marseilles, "a city of Liguria in the land of the Celts". Marseilles had been created around 600 BC and was to become important, facilitating the growth of trade throughout the known world. Part of this growing trade was the transportation of tin from England, which subsequently followed the overland route through France to Marseilles, and from there to anywhere in the known world.

Hecateus spoke of there being a Bardic Tradition in existence among the Celts and he mentioned elaborate Festivals of Music and Dance held by Celtic people on "a Western island" off the coast of Gaul (now France). These Festivals were in honour of Lagh, the Celtic Apollo.

In 1989 I had gone to Iona with Cris Winter where we met with some Druids who were holding a Convention on the island. I was to discover that there were certain religious practices, possibly introduced by Saint Columba himself, which had existed until the fifteenth or sixteenth centuries. These practices were brought to an end by Christian Orthodoxy.

Each year people from Iona, the Isle of Mull and mainland Argyll would meet at the foot of *Dun I*, the highest point of the island. This probably had a lot to do with the giant rose quartz crystal we found, partly-buried, not far from the base of the highest point. We believed at the time that it would have originally been situated on the summit of *Dun I*, having been removed some time later.

The author (John Houston) believes that Saint Columba had introduced to Caledonia or Pictland a Religion which worshipped the Celtic Apollo or else Ion, the Son of Apollo with *Iona* where Saint Columba's monastery was built being named *as such* in honour of Ion, the Son of Apollo. They would have made extensive use of crystals.

(10) For quite some time after *Saturn's Return*, which happens every 29.46 years, when Saturn is in the heavens where it was, approximately, at the time of the birth experience, the author (John Houston) had dreams and visions in which the word *AOS* would appear.

Usually it would appear at the end of a dream when a teacher would write *AOS* on a blackboard and then I would leave school. My best friend at secondary school would also appear.

In 1982, I had gone to Glasgow University and to the Department of Celtic Languages to look into the origins of the word *AOS*. Later on, as I walked down Sauchiehall Street towards the Central Station for a train to East Kilbride, *a vision came to me*. In the vision I was seated on the back seat of a car, being driven through mountainous terrain. I could also see a loch which stretched for miles.

The car slowed down. It veered to the right, then to the left and again it veered to the right as it headed downhill towards the loch. A farmhouse became visible. The car stopped outside the farmhouse and someone said "you had better tell them that John is here". With this, the vision ended.

The word *AOS* is indeed ancient and there were attempts in the seventeenth century to establish a genre of official clan poets, using the vernacular. These people were known as *An t-AOS Dana*; being considered to be orators, the *AOS Dana* were held in high esteem.

The *AOS Dana* were viewed as gifted people, as an intelligentsia. They were trained in Classical Gaidhlig for matters pertaining to the Celtic world and in Latin for international relations.

In 1986 I was invited to Rynachulaig, a farm in mid-Perthshire owned by Andrew James Collingwood, my great friend and mentor. All in all my Rynachulaig years lasted from 1986 until 1999.

I *recognised* the farm from the vision which had come to me four years earlier, although the vision seen in 1982 has *yet* to be fulfilled. The circumstances relating to my arrival at the farm were different.

After a communal meal I went down to the shore of Loch Tay and lit a fire. There with Earth, Water, Fire and Air in abundance, I asked for a sign. As I walked up the side of the hill which led to the farmhouse I saw the sign. *It was a peacock feather on a Scottish Thistle.* That which is symbolic of Krishna rested on *one* of Scotland's greatest symbols.

At the time, for me, this only highlighted the fact that I had been guided by Lord Krishna with the author (John Houston) having seen the thousand-petalled lotus of Krishna in January 1980 at the time of Saturn's Return. Thereafter the writings started to come *to* me.

From the time of my first visit to the farm I had heard that a ghostly choir could be heard, although only rarely. On Midsummer's Day, in 1991, Madison (my partner at the time) and I *heard* the choir.

As a word *AOS* is interesting; it relates to Time, or to do with the passage of Time. This can be seen in words such as *Aosda*, which means 'aged' or 'antiquated'; *Aosmhor* means 'ancient'; if someone were to be asked their age, the word used would be *Aois*.

In the late 60s my family received a letter from a New Zealand kinsman, named James Houston. In the letter he mentioned that the Houston symbol was the hourglass and our motto was 'Time'.

(11) In the earliest of days the Kings of Scots were buried on Iona; some may even have been buried on an island in Loch Awe, in Argyll. In due course the Kings and Queens of Scots were to be crowned at Scone, in Perthshire. This would have been after the union of the Scots and the Picts under the Kingship of Kenneth MacAlpine.

Kenneth I, King of Scots, succeeded his father, Albyn, as King in 841 AD. By 843 AD Kenneth MacAlpine had won the support of the

Picts, enabling the foundation of a united Scots Kingdom north of the river Clyde and the river Forth. The centre of the Church left Iona for the Court at Dunkeld.

This may have been due to extensive folklore pertaining, in part, to *a yew tree* at Fortingall in mid-Perthshire. No one can say how old it is but some say that it is the oldest living thing on the planet.

In his interesting and informative book, *Warriors of the Word*, Michael Newton (on page 238, from the chapter, *Belief Systems and Cosmology*), informs us that:

> There are a number of trees in Scotland that were sacred in pre-Christian times, sometimes close to a place name containing the early Celtic term *nemeton*, 'sacred site', or a later derivative. Most notable of these is the yew at Fortingall, thought to be between three and five thousand years old, which is near the *nemeton* name 'Duneaves', and the traditional centre of Scotland.

Prince Charles Edward Stuart may have been making his way there after the collapse of the Jacobite Cause in 1746. He may have been doing this in order to perform magic rituals for the regaining of the Scots Throne for the Stuarts.

All Gaidhlig students have an opportunity to read *The Books of Clanranald*, in which mention is made of Prince Charles Edward Stuart, who was in the vicinity of Aberfeldy, not far from Fortingall. The Prince was told to look out for a man who had a pouch around his neck. This was to be the one who would lead him westwards through the Highlands and to a French ship and safety.

Nearby at the time there was a young man from the Isle of Skye. His name was Donald Ban MacCrimmon and he bore a remarkable similarity to Prince Charles Edward Stuart, so much so in fact that when two Redcoats spotted Donald Ban, they went to arrest him.

In an act of great selflessness Donald Ban MacCrimmon *pretended* to be the Prince and, when he fell mortally wounded after a sword fight, screamed at them: "You fools! You have killed your king!" This further enabled the Prince to make his escape.

When word reached the family of Donald Ban there was great sadness; his family were, themselves, the legendary pipers to the MacLeods of Dunvegan. Padraig Mor MacCrimmon picked up his pipes and, as though by instinct, he started to play one of the greatest and most haunting laments of all, *The Lament for Donald Ban MacCrimmon*.

(12) We have seen how Pythagoras worshipped Apollo, revering Apollo above all others. There were a variety of Cults and Sects all dedicated to the worship of Apollo, the worship of Apollo being spread far and wide by the Ionians, who also venerated Ion, the Son of Apollo.

It was stated that Apollo worshipped the Hyperborean Apollo. The Hyperboreans, according to Greek Myth, lived in the extreme north, beyond the North Wind, in a sunny land which, it was claimed, Apollo once visited. Legend also states that these Hyperboreans lived exceptionally long lives.

This could give us ground for belief that the original worship of Apollo spread southwards towards the Greeks and Ionians who fashioned it further for their own convenience.

It existed in the British Isles as was witnessed by Hecateus, who mentions elaborate Festivals of Music and Dance in honour of the Celtic Apollo. Perhaps this Celtic Apollo was Ion.

What could have been meant by the use of the term 'Hyperborean'? Its use, as we have seen, was in reference to a Civilisation of sorts which existed in "the extreme north, beyond the North Wind". The worship of Apollo may have originated there.

This would have been the area from which the remnants of UR III emanated around 3000 BC. Archaeologists have uncovered remains of villages and so on with the evidence uncovered indicating that the people were light-skinned and they seem to have used for their outer garments a cloth which was multi-coloured, not unlike *a Scottish tartan*.

Those Ancient Scots who came to the British Isles did not wear tartan; indeed their colour was saffron, denoting Sun worship. They imposed their culture upon the Caledonians or Picts, these being the people who wore tartan. In due course the Ancient Scots were to be assimilated into Scotland and those great Clan chiefs, who would boast of their Ancient Ancestors, were also proud to wear the tartan of the Clan it represented.

The *indigenous* people of the British Isles, that is, those people who were resident in the British Isles *before* the arrival of Gaeldom *en masse*, like other ancient peoples, had a tendency to use *triads* as fundamental to their linguistic expressiveness.

This is true of Hebrew where words formed pertaining to a word such as 'writing' used the triad *k,t,b*. The verb 'to write' is *katab*, whereas 'writer' would be *koteb*.

The Old Testament was composed of the Books of Moses, known as the Torah, the Nebi'im or Prophets and the Kethubim, the Writings. Kethubim, as we might expect, is based on the triad *k,t,b*.

The earliest people to have lived in the British Isles used the triad *w,l,s*. The earliest known system of names in the British Isles are variations of the triad *w,l,s*.

It is for this reason that we have place names such as *Wales*; there are surnames such as Welsh and Walsh, undoubtedly one of the oldest Irish names. Then there is Wills, Willis with Wilkes and Willetts, Wells and Walls, with Wallis and Wallace in addition to this.

What might that have to do with this Northern Land of the Hyperboreans? Archaeologists have uncovered information about Constantinople, formerly known as Byzantium; its earliest known name was Walesa which is founded on the triad *w,l,s*.

Those Hyperborean peoples who had headed south out of necessity due to climate change, a movement of people which would have led to the end of UR III, would themselves have been pushed further and further westwards over the centuries to come.

The existence of such people, from whom the Western Gauls were descended, has left evidence of their settlements in the Middle East as well as Asia Minor.

There is a *Galatti* in Romania; there is a *Galaasiya* in Uzbekistan; there is a *Galaymore* and a *Galkynys* in Turkmenistan; there is a *Galeh Dar* in Iran; there is a *Gali* in Georgia; there is a *Gallipoli* and a *Galatia* in Turkey; there is a *Galatina* in Italy and *Galicia* in Spain. France was once known as *Gaul* and there are vestiges in the name *Portugal*.

In Ireland there are place names such as *Galway* and there is *Donegal*; in Scotland there is *Galloway* and, in Gaidhlig, the Scottish Lowlands is referred to as *Galldachd*, or as *Am Machair Gallda*.

Fingal's Cave was known as such because of *Fingal*, 'the fair-haired Gall', and there are names such as *MacDougall*, 'son of the black-haired Gall'.

10: The Unfolding Vision

There will be *no need* for belief in either Jesus Christ or the prophet Muhammed in the future. They were both central characters in the propagation of a Royal Lie, *Someone* for the uneducated to believe in. This should never alter the fact that Religion should be respected for it can sustain hope; indeed, in previous generations, the Religious Authorities provided the *only* education there was, this provision being well-intentioned.

It is for this reason that those who turn to *The Cult of Jesus Christ* or to Islam in the hope of encountering Divine Revelation will be disappointed. Neither the Christian Faith nor Islam reveal anything substantial about the nature of the Godhead. Such Knowledge requires Initiation.

Fundamental to the Royal Lie was belief in a *Creator* God, whom both Jesus and Muhammed proclaimed. Fundamental to the proclamations of the Christian Faith and Islam was that it was through either Jesus or Muhammed that we were able to know the nature and purpose of this Creator God. The Royal Lie merely encouraged *belief* but it did not and could not offer *Knowledge*.

Today we can grasp the Truth that God is *not* the Creator God of old but rather it is God who is *being created*. How can this be the case?

If God is to exist then this requires the Acquisition of the Divine Identity. This is the good end of the process we refer to as Life which is only possible because our Ultimate Ancestor is predisposed to exist and, therefore, *will* exist *no* matter what. The process of the attainment of the Divine Identity necessarily involves a *Human* stage in this process of Deification.

The Godhead *arises from* the Human Race. *If* the Ultimate Ancestor can assume Human form by *incarnating* on Earth then, thereby, the Ultimate Ancestor can *reproduce* Itself on Earth. By means of the Human Race the Ultimate Ancestor can assume Its Identity within the context of the Identity of a Collective Consciousness, such as Humanity.

God therefore evolves *by means of* the Human Race. From being One it will become Many enabling the Godhead to interact with Itself, as It and only It actually exists, being the Source of everything.

The fulfilment of the Divine quest for the Divine Identity is achieved by following *The Uncreated Vision*; in the coming to pass of *The Uncreated Vision* the Destiny of God is realised. This Vision is the means of *guiding* the Ultimate Ancestor to Its Self-Realisation *as* the One and *as* the All.

'In the beginning' there was Predisposition which was to become Self-Aware. This Self-Experience *of* the Predisposition to *be* God was as the Divine Archetype.

The Archetype, in experiencing the Infinite Possibility *of* the Predisposition to *be* God *became* the Ultimate Ancestor of All. This was brought about by the Archetype experiencing the *necessity* of compliance with the Predisposition to *be* or to *become* God. Such Predisposition *requires* compliance.

The Ultimate Ancestor was called into existence due to the necessity of the Self-Expression of the Predisposition to be God. Predisposition, once experienced, *must* express Itself.

The Ultimate Ancestor, by means of Existence, *manifests* the Predisposition *of* God to *be* God. It is a *personal* experience. Not only that but it is also the fulfilment of a Vision. By means of the Thought Process of the Human Race, the Vision is apprehended and Humanity brings the Vision to completion. The Human Race exists for this Purpose.

In experiencing the Predisposition *of* God to *be* or to *become* God, the Ultimate Ancestor, as the *Expression* of the Divine Predisposition, embarks upon a Process, the purpose of which is *Personalisation* for the sake of the Acquisition of Identity.

The Uncreated Vision, which has been ordained to come to pass, will guide the Ultimate Ancestor; indeed the good end of the existence of the Ultimate

Ancestor is that the Ultimate Ancestor should live according to Its nature, which is *as* a Collective Consciousness.

The Uncreated Vision will guide the Ultimate Ancestor from being One to becoming 'the One amongst the Many'. The good end of *The Uncreated Vision* is the One being able to *manifest* Itself *as* the Supreme Personality of Godhead.

With the Self-Realisation of *The Uncreated Vision*, the One becomes the Supreme Personality of Godhead. The One and the All experiences Self-expression *as* a Collective Consciousness. This is also the Self-Realisation of that *Uncreated Vision* which is *predestined* to come to pass.

Here we need to remind ourselves that none of this would be possible without Predisposition, indeed Predisposition is the Only Reality. Nothing can happen without Predisposition.

The Realisation of Destiny, the coming into Reality of *The Uncreated Vision*, is only the outworking of Predisposition towards Its *Predestined* Self-Realisation, *as* the One and *as* the All.

11: Creating the Divine Identity

God is predisposed to exist. This is the reason why Life is possible, indeed the Predisposition *of* God to *be* God is the foundation of *all* Life.

The Self-experience of the Predisposition to be God was expressed as the Archetype who became the Ultimate Ancestor of all. This means that the Archetype was *the effect* of the Self-experience and subsequent means for the Self-expression of God. The Archetype was *how* the Self-expression of the Predisposition to be God was made *possible*.

Our Thought Processes are the equivalent of an *Uncreated Vision*. This *Uncreated Vision* is the driving force of Life. It must be *apprehended* – indeed the existence of the Human Race is for the sake of this apprehension. *The Uncreated Vision* must create the circumstances for Its own Self-Realisation *as* the Universal Self, God as a Collective Consciousness. By this means Cosmic Consciousness is *assured*.

The growth of complexity in Nature is *the means* of Self-development or evolution of *The Uncreated Vision*. It is a Process. It is actually a Biological Process. The growth of complexity in Nature, the Self-expression of Predisposition, is *the means* of awakening the Sub-Personalities of Godhead who presently exist *as* Human beings on planet Earth.

The Uncreated Vision, as an expression of *The Unlimited*, is the means for the Creation of the Divine Identity; the Divine Identity is *The Limit*. The Process goes from Allness and the Absolute *to* Particulars. Thereby we may be able to *recognise* the One amongst the Many. This is also the growth of complexity in Nature.

The Archetype, from whom the Ultimate Ancestor emanated as an Expression *of* the Archetype, is *predisposed* to exist and, accordingly, *will* exist no matter what. The Human Race is descended from a Person who will exist, with everything that exists an Extension of the Personality of Godhead.

The Reality is the Self-Realisation of the Predisposition to exist as the Universal Self. This Universal Self is the *outcome* of the Self-experience of the Predisposition to be God as initially experienced *by* the Ultimate Ancestor *as* the Ultimate Ancestor.

As the Universal Self, God is replete with a myriad of sub-personalities; God is no longer a Singularity. The Ultimate Ancestor now seeks to *appear* or to be made manifest *as* the Supreme Personality of Godhead.

The task is the *awakening* of the Universal Self to Gnosis, a Gnosis about the Divine Identity as a Collective Consciousness. The fullness of Life is to be experienced as a Collective Consciousness. The Godhead, from being One, has become a *Relationship*. It is this Relationship which is now the Divine Identity.

The Self-development of the Godhead is made possible by means of the Human Race, the source of all Wisdom and Power.

Abstraction becomes Existent by means of the requirement of experiencing an existence which can provide the Possibility for *Incarnation*. The Collective Consciousness requires the provision of Particulars for the sake of Recognition; this is so because, as a Collective Consciousness we may have to recognise a speciality in others.

Although each one comes into existence *already* equipped to do something with *excellence*, the purpose of this is that we may be able to supplement and complement each other, quite *naturally*. Although being Many we may be able to operate *as* One.

12: The Necessity of Incarnation

Incarnation is for the *Necessity* of gaining Knowledge which comes *as* Recollection; our Ultimate Ancestor, through Incarnation, *seeks to remember* Itself as the embodiment of the Predisposition *of* God to *be* God. The Ultimate Ancestor is thereby empowered to reproduce Itself as a Collective Consciousness.

The task of our Ultimate Ancestor is to bring to life a *Recollection* of that Divine Predisposition from which we originate and which will permit the *appearance* of the Ultimate Ancestor *as* the Supreme Personality of Godhead.

This *Rebirth,* as a *Recollection* of the Divine Origin, must happen *if* the Predisposition of God to be God is to be able to express Itself, or *manifest* Itself. Incarnation is about this Appearance, about this Manifestation, and Manifestation *as* a Collective Consciousness.

This Appearance or Manifestation of our *Suprahistorical Ancestor* (1), when witnessed by Humanity, in accordance with Esoteric Tradition, is referred to as the One known as either Hermes Trismegistus, or as Ion, the Son of Apollo. This happens when we recognise intuitively that this Hermes or this Ion are actually at *One* with their Divine Origin, thereby *expressing* It.

That Original State of Consciousness was, in effect, the Self-experience of the Divine Predisposition to be God. Its Self-Experience was as the Archetype; Its Self-Expression was *as* the Ultimate Ancestor.

From being Allness and Absolute the Godhead seeks a Divine Identity for Self-Expression; prior to this, in consequence of being Allness and Absolute, the Godhead was only an *Abstraction*. The Self-expression of that Divine Predisposition to be God *demanded* Change and, as has been touched upon in *The Sacred Ibis Speaks*, only that which is material *can* change.

It is about Manifestation, about Form, about Experiencing, about Witnessing. This is so because Knowledge is required. Memory *requires* Recollection to gain Knowledge. This Recollection, according to Esoteric Tradition, *requires* the Human Race, *as* Racial Memory, being the source of all Wisdom and Power.

The Evolution of Consciousness is the Evolution of the Human Race. The Evolution of the Human Race (*as* Racial Memory) is the Evolution of the ability to recall the Divine Origin and, as such, the Human Race is *predisposed* to operate as the source of *all* Wisdom and Power.

Recollection is where Mind and Matter conspire. Humanity is *the* means of Recollection. Memory is not an end in Itself, but for the awakening of Predisposition. It is fundamental to a necessary *interim* stage.

The Ultimate Ancestor seeks to be incarnated as the Supreme Personality of Godhead. This is the expression of the Absolute, or *The Unlimited* within the preset *Limit*, within the context of which there is an unfolding of the Divine Necessity to *reproduce*, to express Itself as a Collective Consciousness.

The Limit demands proportion; perfect proportion is perfect beauty. This Person is All-Attractive, indeed physically attractive to an unlimited degree. This is Hermes, the beautiful express image of the Heavenly father. This is Krishna whose name means *Attraction*. This is Apollo, of elegant physique and a countenance of perfect beauty.

The Supreme Personality of Godhead is the First and the Last, the Beginning and End of everything. All striving is for the manifestation of this appearance for, without this Appearance, there would be *nothing*.

NOTES

(1) This Suprahistorical Ancestor of the Human Race is always depicted as being a fabulous Musician; the Ancient Scots, like other branches of the

Human family viewed Music as being *magical*, capable of bridging the gap between Humanity and the gods. Hermes, Orpheus and Apollo are all depicted as being beautiful as well as playing the *lyre*.

There is evidence to suggest that the lyre existed within Gaeldom from the earliest of times. Other instruments were played although we should note that the clarsach (the harp) came later, probably in the seventh century, the fiddle from around 1000 AD and the bagpipes from the thirteenth century. These dates are only estimates at best.

The lyre, well-known from Ancient times, probably developed from periods of interaction with the Greeks and would have been associated with the Cults of Apollo or of Ion.

Archaeologists have uncovered the probable remains of lyres in various places but the lyre, due to its connection with remote Antiquity, went out of favour with the introduction of *The Cult of Jesus Christ.*

13: Through History to Remembrance

The Archetype, being the Self-experience of the Predisposition to *be* God or to *become* God, became the Ultimate Ancestor of All that *is*. There is only *one* Life, the Life *of* God.

Within the Milky Way, the Sun was to produce the Earth whilst the Earth produced the Human Race and all in consequence of the Predisposition-driven Growth of Complexity in Nature. This is a Process the *predestined* end of which is the creation of circumstances for *Manifestation*, the Manifestation of the Ultimate Ancestor *as* the Supreme Personality of Godhead.

The Human Race exists to facilitate the Self-realisation of this Process, whereby *The Uncreated Vision* comes to pass. In the unfolding of the Vision by means of *us*, we are only acting in accordance with the *Necessity* of our Nature. We *must* comply with our Predisposition.

The Predisposition-driven life force exists to guide us to the Realisation of the Manifestation of our Ultimate Ancestor. Everything that exists will, unwittingly if need be, comply with the Predisposition which is attracted to make *manifest* the Supreme Personality of Godhead, the Son of God, Hermes Trismegistus or Krishna, or Ion, the Son of Apollo.

We must evolve still further; this is a *Necessity* but the Necessity of our further evolution is *not* our own Necessity. Our further evolution is what drives

Hermes onwards from Age to Age. It is for Hermes to awaken or quicken Humanity in anticipation of a Great Rebirth for Humanity, a Quantum Leap in terms of Consciousness.

It is for the Supreme Personality of Godhead to awaken *us*. Hermes is the means for *our* awakening. Hermes will do this for *us*.

The Godhead has been clothed in Matter, or Artificial Intelligence, for the sake of *Recollection*. It seeks to remember Its Divine Origin. With that Recollection, as a Gnosis, the Divine Origin which is a level of Consciousness, is *Reborn* as the manifestation of the Supreme Personality of Godhead.

Matter is Memory and through Matter, by means of a growing Recollection, the Godhead will be *empowered* to experience Its own History as It remembers who It is and, accordingly, what is Its Predisposition.

The Manifestation of the Supreme Personality of Godhead is the *Rebirth* of the Original Predisposition to be God. A change has occurred and only that which is Material can change.

The Predisposition to be God has been manifested for the sake of Reproduction. The Archetype, who became the Ultimate Ancestor, is now able to Reproduce *Itself* by means of the Human Race.

The result of this is that Humanity becomes more evolved, more God-like. Hermes is deifying the Human Race by means of generation. Hermes has reproduced Himself here for the purpose of the eventual creation of a Human Race which is *fully* Divine, like Hermes or Ion.

When the Human Race has become more evolved, the message implicit in the New Testament, which is that the Earth *belongs as an inheritance* to a Prince from another world, will come to fruition.

This will herald the arrival of those Beings who are from the world of the New Testament Angels. They will intermarry and thereby cross-fertilise with the New Humanity on Earth.

14: Predisposition & Necessity

From the time of the Greek philosophers there has been a preoccupation with the so-called Dualism of Mind and Matter. For the author (John Houston) it is more realistic to think of this Dualism as the relationship formed out of the interplay between Predisposition and Necessity.

As has been mentioned in previous chapters it is *Predisposition* which makes everything possible with life, as we know it, being the outcome of the Predisposition of the Ultimate Ancestor to *become* God. Not even an Omnipotent God can come into existence fully developed. It must evolve.

From the Archetype, who was the Original Self-awareness of the Predisposition of God to be or to *become* God, the Ultimate Ancestor appeared *as* the Self-expression of the Predisposition to create the Divine Identity for the *manifestation* of the Divine Attributes, as the Personality of Godhead.

Predisposition and Necessity are both Modes of Action within the All. This interplay is the context within which Life appears and evolves, resulting in the Growth of Complexity in Nature.

Because of Predisposition, Life necessarily has *Purpose*. The Ultimate Ancestor, known now as Hermes Trismegistus or as Ion, the Son of Apollo, seeks to realise this Purpose as it is integrally involved with Hermes' quest for the Acquisition of the Divine Identity. Hermes is actually seeking to create the means for Recollection of His Divine Origin.

Initially Hermes, or Ion, know nothing. Through undergoing a Process of Purification, Hermes or Ion arrive at a Knowledge of Self *as* the Supreme Personality of Godhead, which is the True Identity.

It is here that we realise that Hermes requires us, as Human beings, for the Self-regulation or Self-purification of Hermes. It is through *us* and through *interaction with us* that Hermes or Ion is purified. In the increased Activation of the Human Race to an Awakening of Knowledge or Gnosis, Hermes is also, at the same time, awakening Himself.

In this Process of the Deification of Hermes we, too, are awakened to our Divinity. This is something which Hermes must do for us but which, at the same time, Hermes is doing for Hermes. The reason for this is quite straightforward: Hermes *cannot* emerge as the Supreme Personality of Godhead without the Emanations being able to *consciously relate* to Hermes.

In dealing with and, to an extent, overcoming Necessity on the path of gaining Self-Knowledge Hermes is learning, or remembering, what it *means* to be Hermes.

Hermes has been incarnated here from another world, the world of the Biblical Angels. Through Hermes the Consciousness of the world of the Biblical Angels is able to interact with the Consciousness of the planet Earth to become One. Tradition relates to us that this is *why* the Human Race exists.

Hermes has been incarnated here for the sake of the Recollection of His Divine Origin; for Hermes this is a Necessity for the *becoming* of Hermes.

In the Recollection of the Divine Origin, as a State of Consciousness, Hermes is *awakened* to and as such becomes the Identity of the Divine Origin; this is a *Necessity* for Hermes in as much as this is what Hermes is *Predisposed* to do.

In the Recollection of His Divine Origin, Hermes is thereby equipped to live according to His nature. Hermes will be able to manifest Himself, to the glory of God, *as* the Supreme Personality of Godhead.

This will cause great excitement among those Emanations who are an extension of His Personality.

In Recollecting His Divine Origin by means of Incarnation, Hermes or Ion is thereby equipped to *Reproduce* in accordance with Predisposition. Through this interaction with Humanity, Hermes is able to live in accordance with His nature and the Human Race will produce offspring which, with each successive Incarnation are equipped, by means of generation, to become more Divine, *more like* Hermes or Ion, who is also the Ultimate Ancestor.

Through such Incarnations the Human Race becomes increasingly Divine, as a reflection of the Divine Archetype, who became the Ultimate Ancestor. As this process continues eventually Humanity will be able to reach a level of Consciousness which can cross-fertilise with the world of the Biblical Angels.

The Truth of the Esoteric Tradition which is the *undercurrent* of the Western Philosophical Tradition is that, after having created the Divine Humanity, which is the Destiny of the Human Race, the Biblical Angels will be able to take up residence on Earth where they will reproduce themselves by means of the Divine Humanity.

Humanity, as we have known It, will be no more for It will have become assimilated into the Civilisation of the Biblical Angels; on Earth a Kingdom will exist 'until times indefinite'.

All of this will take place with Hermes *remembering* that He is operating as a Necessary Being and that, as a Necessary Being, He must live according to His nature.

Hermes will be driven on from world to world, from Age to Age, doing that which He is *predisposed* to do, to be reproduced as a Collective Consciousness which will be fully Divine as Hermes is.

Herein there is a great Truth; even Hermes Trismegistus has to live in accordance with Predisposition. Whatever *Necessities* Hermes has encountered on the path of Self-Realisation or Self-Recollection, they have all acted, in the final analysis, *to guide* Hermes to the Realisation of Destiny.

Necessity is such that it triggers the Self-Expression of Predisposition. Nothing can thwart the work of God. The irresistible Predisposition for the sake of which we exist will lead, eventually, to the Recollection of the Divine Origin, and to Hermes producing a Race of Beings who, like Hermes, are *not only predisposed* to recall their Divine Origin but are *fully* able to do so.

From the Human chrysalis the psychic butterflies will emerge for the continuance of Life on an endless basis; in so doing the Divine Humanity is existing as the *embellished* Expression of the Predisposition of God to become God, to do what God is predisposed to do.

Eternal interplay between the Supreme Personality of Godhead and the sub-personalities, who are Extensions of that Supreme Personality, will be the outcome. This is the fulfilment of *The Uncreated Vision*. Predisposition has gained Absolute Self-Expression.

15: The Mystery Explained

There was Predisposition.

Predisposition undergoes Self-experience.

The Predisposition is experienced as *The Archetype*, an Archetypal Pattern; thus the Self-experience of the Predisposition *of* God to *be* God was rendered possible.

The Self-experience of the Predisposition to be God would produce the Ultimate Ancestor who came into existence *as* the Self-Expression of the eternal Predisposition of God to be God.

The Ultimate Ancestor, being *Predisposed* to become the Supreme Personality of Godhead, must awaken what will appear as Sub-Personalities to satisfy the urgings of Its Predisposition to become the Supreme Personality of Godhead.

The birth of the Universe, as we know it, was *not* the Beginning 'that once was'. The 'Big Bang' was *not* the cause of the universe but the initial *effect* of that which made the existence of the Universe possible; the Predisposition of God to be God produced the 'Big Bang', thereby initiating a Process.

The 'Big Bang' was the Initial Manifestation of a Process, the good end of which is the Creation of the Divine Identity.

The Universe has Its origin in the Predisposition *of* God to *become* God.

The Universe is the *Extension* of the Personality of Godhead; the Human Race is also an Extension of the Supreme Personality of Godhead for through Humanity the Divine Predisposition may be expressed.

The Divine Identity will be the Identity which *corresponds* to the Predisposition of God to be God; as such, it will have to mirror the Archetypal Pattern which was the *Self-experience* of the Godhead's Predisposition to be God.

This is why Form is essential, for Change must happen.

In the Acquisition of Form, *as* an Identity, the Ultimate Ancestor is transformed from being an Abstraction to experiencing Existence.

Only that which is Material can render Change possible.

From being One, a Singularity, the Ultimate Ancestor is now predisposed to *appear*, to be made *manifest* as the Supreme Personality of Godhead.

All Manifestation is actually the Manifestation of the *necessity* of one's Nature.

It would be a mistake to think that, somehow or other, the One is now no longer One; It experiences Itself as 'One *amongst* the Many'.

The Change which has occurred has been in relation to the *Expression of Form*; the fundamental Predisposition has not changed and It never will.

There is only One Person in the Universe.

There is only one Life, this being the Life of God.

From Allness and Absolute and, thereby, from being an Abstraction, the Supreme Personality will witness the Growth of Complexity in nature on unto Infinite Complexity.

The Supreme Personality seeks to transform the Many, as Emanations of the Ultimate Ancestor, into the *likeness* of the Supreme Personality of Godhead.

The task is for the Ultimate Ancestor to be able to express Itself as a Collective Consciousness.

This, as it happens, is the only way for the Ultimate Ancestor to be able to relate to Itself as It, and *only* It, actually exists.

The Infinite seeks to express Itself although It can only do this by *finite* means.

As Existent, the Ultimate Ancestor evolves in terms of Consciousness.

With the attainment of Cosmic Consciousness, which the Ultimate Ancestor experiences as an Awakening, a Transformation occurs, in accordance with Predisposition.

Such Recollection transforms the Ultimate Ancestor into the Supreme Personality of Godhead.

The Acquisition of the Identity of the Supreme Personality of Godhead is for the Purpose of Incarnation.

The *purpose* of the Incarnation is that the Supreme Personality of Godhead, being *the* true Self-expression of the *Original Archetype*, is able to *reproduce* Itself.

It is able to reproduce Itself by means of the Human Race; in being made *manifest* on Earth and Incarnating, Human beings, as Emanations of the Ultimate Ancestor, can be awakened to the Realisation that their true Identity, although Many, *is* the Ultimate Ancestor.

This is so because there is only one Life, the Life of God, which is Predisposition, Itself.

If a Being is to continue to exist then It will have to satisfy those urgings which relate to the *Necessity* of Its nature.

In the case of the Human Race It must ultimately be able to remember Its Divine Origin.

The Relationship of Godhead must be able to continue to exist; not only will the Human Race be aware of Its total reliance upon Predisposition but, inevitably, It will have to be totally subsumed by Predisposition.

Predisposition may thereby experience Transcendence.

The Human Race, which exists as the means of equipping the Supreme Personality of Godhead to express Itself as a Collective Consciousness, has as Its Destiny, a state of existence which will be able to continue on an *endless* basis.

The only Change will be that the One has *appeared* to become the Many.

The Human Race, which is the source of all Wisdom and Power, will become a Collective Consciousness which, just like the Ultimate Ancestor of old, will be able to live on an endless basis as Its Predisposition *dictates*.

Whatever environment we require to continue to exist will appear as an Extension of our Predisposition to exist on an endless basis.

Predisposition will always exist; indeed Predisposition can do nothing other than exist as It *must* express Itself.

Whatever was possible for the Ultimate Ancestor will also be possible for the Collective Consciousness which is the Human Race.

The Many can now express the Divine Attributes of the Ultimate Ancestor.

Mission accomplished.

16: The Law of Moses

From the Old Testament, and from *The Book of Exodus* chapter 20, we read:

And God spoke all these words saying,
I am the Lord your God, who has brought you out of the land of Egypt, out of the land of bondage.
You shall have no other gods before Me.
You shall not make for yourselves any graven images, or any likeness of anything that is in the heavens above or in the Earth beneath, or in the water under the Earth:
You shall not bow down to them, nor serve them; for I, the Lord your God, am a jealous God, visiting the iniquity of the fathers upon the children unto the third and fourth generation of them that hate Me;
And showing mercy unto thousands of them that love Me, and keep My commandments.
You shall not take the name of the Lord your God in vain; for the Lord will not hold them guiltless that take His name in vain.
Remember the Sabbath Day, to keep it holy.
Six days you shall labour thereby doing all your work;

But the seventh day is the Sabbath of the Lord, your God; in it you shall not work whether you, or your son, or your daughter, your manservant or maidservant, or your cattle, or the stranger that is within your gates.

For in six days the Lord made the heavens and the Earth, the seas, and all that is in them, and rested on the seventh day; wherefore the Lord blessed the Sabbath day, and hallowed it.

Honour your father and mother; that your days may be long upon the land which the Lord your God gives you.

You shall not kill.

You shall not commit adultery.

You shall not steal.

You shall not bear false witness against your neighbour.

You shall not covet your neighbour's house, you shall not covet your neighbour's wife, nor his manservant, nor his maidservant, nor his ox, nor his ass, nor anything that is your neighbours.

And all the people saw the thunderings and the lightnings, and the noise of the trumpet, and the mountain smoking; and when all the people saw it, they removed and stood afar off.

And they said unto Moses; speak with us and we will hear; but let not God speak with us lest we die.

17: A Personal Perspective

As a young boy in the suburbs of the city of Glasgow in the 1950s, the author (John Houston) attended Sunday School on a regular basis, being introduced to those stories from the Bible at an early age. In the Biblical narratives, the figure of Moses was of immense importance. Moses was the one whose task it was to lead the Children of Israel, who had become enslaved in Egypt, to the Promised Land of Canaan.

What is the specific message of the Law of Moses for us today at this particular point in Time, an Epochal Threshold, the ending of one Age and the dawning of another Age?

A short commentary on the twentieth chapter of *The Book of Exodus* now follows. What God is depicted as saying to the people of Israel *through* Moses was;

I am the Lord your God, who brought you out of the land of Egypt, out of the house of bondage.

The most important thing for people to realise is that *God* is the author of *all* circumstances; indeed everything that happens does so within a *context*, that context being the *God* Process (1).

From 'the Big Bang' around 13.7 billion years ago and then, from the birth of the planet Earth with the appearance of the Monera, then the Protists, God has been the author of *all* those circumstances. Everything that has happened to us has done so because we are *extensions* of the Personality of Godhead. Our lives *happen to us* within the context of the *unfolding* of the God Process (2).

The narratives in the Bible which pertain to the life and times of Moses, the great Prophet and Servant of God, exist within the context of seeking to explain the significance of the fact that God is the Author of *all* circumstances. Those Children of Israel are assured that whatever course their lives had taken, *God* had been guiding them. Their journey had been pre-destined and pre-ordained by God.

This is intended to clear the decks for the realisation of something very important, which is this: *there is a stage after this*. The Human Race is a gateway, an Exodus from the past. Entering upon that stage of Existence is the Destiny of the Human Race.

When Moses appears on the scene of Time he does not go to the children of Israel to merely give them a précis of their history after which he bids them a fond farewell. Moses appears for the sake of preparing the Children of Israel for a *further* stage in their sojourn, a different kind of life, somewhere else but all, nonetheless, *ordained* by God.

In *The Greater Mysteries of Egypt*, the sixth and penultimate stage had recognised *the sacred ibis* as its symbol (3). During this sixth and penultimate stage Preparation was given for crossing an abyss. This involved the realisation that what we call Existence is actually *non*-Existence. The aim of the sixth and penultimate stage of *The Greater Mysteries of Egypt* was to prepare for entering True Existence.

As the Ultimate Ancestor seeks to *recollect* Itself as the Supreme Personality of Godhead, thereby, the Ultimate Ancestor can reproduce Itself *as* a Collective Consciousness. The penultimate stage of these Greater Mysteries was the Ultimate Ancestor emerging *from* the Human Race, as the Supreme Personality of Godhead. From the Human chrysalis a butterfly will be produced.

In order to return to that Original Consciousness of Self, the One has to undergo the *Human* experience.

The *Human* stage of this experience is the stage, in the unfolding of the God Process, whereby *Recollection* is possible. A Human being has the potential, indeed the Human being is *predisposed*, to remember the Divine Origin.

It is for this reason that among the philosophers of Antiquity the Human Race was recognised as being the *source* of all wisdom and power. Within the

Human Idea, there is a Predisposition to express the Divine Attributes. If the Ultimate Ancestor of the Human Race is able to *assume* Human Form, then it may be able to *manifest* Itself as the Supreme Personality of Godhead; thus the Ultimate Ancestor *incarnates*. This will lead to the *Reproduction* of the Ultimate Ancestor.

Incarnation is for the purpose of Reproduction. With Incarnation there is the *manifestation* of the Predisposition of God to be or to become God. Such Predisposition, once experienced must be expressed. All life exists *for* the manifestation of Predisposition and *as* the manifestation of Predisposition. There is *no* choice, we must comply with Predisposition.

The God Process is concerned with the One becoming 'the One amongst the Many'. As a Collective Consciousness the Human Race is potentially Divine or, better still, the Predisposition of the Human Race is to become like Hermes, or Krishna or Ion, the Son of Apollo, as a Collective Consciousness. Such a Self-evolving Being could exist on an endless basis.

It is the work of the Ultimate Ancestor to *deify* the Human Race, by means of generation. This is *the* means for the Human Race to become Divine, like Hermes, as a Collective Consciousness.

This is something that the Ultimate Ancestor is doing to suit the purpose of the Ultimate Ancestor; this is something which *happens* to the Human Race. It is not something which we choose, as such, because thereby *we are being created* in the image of the Divine Archetype.

We will be guided, therefore, to our Destination which is our Destiny. We are guided by Predisposition, the Predisposition which we ultimately are and for the sake of the expression of which, we exist.

As was the case with the Children of Israel in those Biblical narratives we, too, are being guided. The direction we need to follow will be revealed *to* us. Those who make it to the Promised Land are those who follow that direction. We have our Pillar of Cloud by day and our Pillar of Fire by night; therefore the *success* of our journey will be assured.

For the One to become 'the One amongst the Many' requires Time, with Time as Process; furthermore, Process expresses the Purposeful passage of Time.

You shall have no other gods before Me.

This could just as easily have been 'there are no gods other than Me', or even, 'God is all there is'. There is only God and the Godhead expresses Itself through the God Process. This is a Relationship of everything that *is*. There is nothing *other* than God and there is nothing *outside* God. Everything exists for the sake of the *manifestation* of the Ultimate Ancestor as the Supreme Personality of Godhead.

This brings us face to face with what was referred to as *The Supreme Secret of the Ancients*, an Ancient Truth about the Human Race and *why* the Human Race exists. It also forces us to encounter the Truth that it is *not* God that we seek but *how* we may be able to exemplify the power of God in our lives. We exist to suit the purpose of God and this is fulfilled when we live according to our nature.

The *purpose* of the Law of Moses was to provide instruction for people. The prophetic community engaged in the provision of this service recognised the need to lower their message to the level of the infirmity of those seeking instruction. Meaningful communication would have been impossible otherwise.

People would have come to the Temple with all sorts of weird and wonderful ideas, all of them founded on Superstition. They would have had no education as we understand the term. Their beliefs would have lacked coherency, being founded upon a mass of those syncretistic aspects of belief drawn from the reservoir of the popular mythology of the day. The Instruction they would receive would be of the most rudimentary stripe, the basics of a process designed to impart Knowledge and inculcate Virtue.

For the author (John Houston) there is *no* such thing as *The True Religion* (4) but there is the true *purpose* of Religion, this being to prepare the aspirant or devotee for Initiation in *The Mysteries* whereby Holy Knowledge (Gnosis) would be revealed. The importance of this is considerable for Knowledge of some kind is the only good (5), indeed those who we recognise as being wise are forever learning, but they are *never* the unlearned (6).

Taking the uneducated to the stage of Initiation into *The Greater Mysteries* of Egypt did happen. It was possible. This would have come in degrees or stages but the purpose remained unaltered. The Human Race has a Destiny *vouchsafed* by God and, through those who are able to receive Instruction, there is the possibility of Knowledge dawning and Destiny being realised.

The prophetic community would have instructed the mass of the population to understand that there is but *one* God, the Divine Ancestor of the Human Race, indeed of *all* life. The prophetic community, furthermore, would have led the aspirants or devotees to the understanding that our Ultimate Ancestor *now* manifests Itself *as* the Human Race. The Knowledge of the

Ultimate Ancestor having assumed Human Form is the sixth or penultimate stage of *The Greater Mysteries* of Egypt.

Those who were to receive Initiation into *The Mysteries* would learn that life as we know it is *only possible* because of Predisposition. The fount of all life is the Predisposition of God to be God. The Human Race exists to create the Divine Identity; indeed the Human Race exists as *the means* of the Creation of the Divine Identity. Humanity as we know it is not yet fully deified.

The *True* Expression of the Godhead will arise *from* the Human Race. The understanding of this is the gift of God. There is *no* God but the One who is the Supreme Personality of Godhead.

> *You shall not make any graven images, or any likeness of anything*
> *that is in the heavens above or in the Earth beneath, or in the water*
> *under the Earth. You shall not bow down to them, nor serve them; for*
> *I, the Lord your God, am a jealous God.*

Ignorance never comes without an accompaniment. It *will* seek to express itself. This usually comes as *fear*, the fear of what others may do or say, the fear of the unknown with its constant uncertainty.

Ignorance is the greatest problem of all; behaviour which we would designate as being *unethical* has its basis in ignorance. The great ignorance which troubles the Human Race is that we are ignorant of the fact that we are the Creation of God, a landmark on the path of creating the Divine Identity as a Collective Consciousness.

At this stage in the evolution of Consciousness, the Human Race is still fundamentally ignorant of Its true nature and of Its powers. This is the true ignorance. This is why the wise Socrates, upon summoning Apollo, was informed that he was to 'know himself'.

Such Knowledge would be the realisation that everything is pre-destined and that the Human Race is, in fact, predisposed to exist *as* the expression of the Divine Attributes. Only that Knowledge can liberate the pilgrim from that restlessness that inclines people towards seeking for Truth. That search only ends with the realisation that God, the Ultimate Ancestor, dwells within us.

In life people often express disappointment because of a lack of progress on the path of spiritual development. They habitually seek out guidance for the uncovering of that remedy which will bring an end to the frustration experienced due to a *perceived* lack of progress.

People therefore support their faith in a whole multitude of ways but all of these are quite unnecessary. People have been found to consult all sorts of soothsayers, for whose services money is exchanged, but their problem is that they are having to contend with ignorance expressed as the failure to recognise that they are *internally* guided.

The *Celtic Mysteries* featured the salmon, whose Gaidhlig name is *Bradan*, the salmon having fascinated Mystics from the very dawn of the Human Race. The reason for this was that the salmon can swim out into the Atlantic Ocean and then, when the time comes, *instinctively* head home. What fascinated the Ancients about the salmon was that the salmon are able to return to their place of origin *without* instruction.

The salmon have no need of Transcendental Meditation to return home; neither do they study the Bible or pray to Jesus or light candles to the Virgin Mary, but they return home *nonetheless*. By the same token, the salmon do not chant Hare Krishna and neither do they pray five times a day in the direction indicated by Mecca.

The ignorance which is so debilitating masks the fact that we are reliant upon Knowledge to fulfil our Destiny, with this Knowledge coming as Recollection. Human beings do not require anything in addition to Human nature for the Human Race exists to make this Holy Knowledge *possible,* as Recollection.

Like the story of the Great Exodus undertaken by Moses, the pilgrim does not need to discover through trial and error the direction to follow for the purpose of reaching the Promised Land. The pilgrim is guided by a Pillar of Cloud by day and a Pillar of Fire by night. *Guidance was provided* for the sake of the Self-Realisation of the Process.

The Godhead is such that, as it states in the New Testament, and from *The Acts of the Apostles*, "in Him we live, in Him we move, in Him we have our being" (7).

> *Visiting the iniquity of the fathers upon the children unto the third and fourth generation of them that hate Me; and showing mercy unto thousands of them that love Me, and keep My commandments.*

In the Ancient World, there were occasions when someone approached the Priesthood of a Temple with questions which, themselves, served as *indicators* that here was someone who had a *natural inclination* towards Initiation into *The Mysteries.*

123

In a sense the aspirant was *identifying* himself, with such inclination serving as an identifying characteristic. Thereafter a Process would begin to assess the suitability of the person *for* Initiation.

Someone who sought Initiation into *The Mysteries* would be expected to prove that they were worthy of Initiation. Such people would have to be diligent, they would have to be prepared to accept responsibility for their actions and, in due course, *they would be judged*, the outcome being that they would fall into one of two categories. They would prove to be either suitable or unsuitable.

From the dawn of Humanity it was evident that there were different types of Human being. There were those whose lives were virtuous, to the extent that their Humanity approached Divinity. On the other hand, however, there were others who lived like animals. By the same token, some Humans were great artists, musicians and singers who would be able to inspire others and, yet again, there were other people who were either unwilling or incapable of overcoming brutish tendencies. Such people cannot be civilised and, accordingly, cannot enter the Kingdom.

The message of the Bible is that a Day of Judgement is coming and that the purpose of the Day of Judgement is to divide the Human Race into *two* groups. Those who are suitable will enter the Kingdom of God which will exist 'until times indefinite', whilst the others will have reached the end of their evolution. After a few generations almost all of them will be gone.

What makes the difference between these two groups is their suitability; as to whether someone is suitable or not will be a value judgement by the Great Shepherd. What is the criterion for suitability?

Suitability will pertain to the ability of a person to evolve *further*, beyond the Human stage as we understand it. Suitability, from the stand point of the aspirant, will depend on the understanding that the aspirant's life does not and never did belong to the aspirant but to the Ultimate Ancestor, who has been fashioning Humanity in accordance with the Archetypal Image which the Ultimate Ancestor is *predisposed* to express for the sake of Reproduction.

The suitability of the aspirant will express itself as the aspirant understanding that he must now *surrender* his life to the will of God for the purpose of fulfilling the *Purpose* of God. Suitability is, therefore, attraction towards *disinterested* activity; suitability is the expression of the recognition that the wellbeing of the Kingdom is of greater importance than any so-called individual rights or privileges; suitability is expressed in the desire to *serve*.

You shall not take the name of the Lord your God in vain; for the Lord will not hold them guiltless that take His name in vain.

This surely brings us back to the Realisation that God is the author of *all* our circumstances. The Human Race exists as *the* means of the Self-Expression of the Godhead. The Human Race has a Purpose, but this Purpose is *not* our own Purpose for it is God's Purpose and God has the Human Race for the outworking of God's Purpose.

Human beings exist as Extensions of the Personality of Godhead. The existence of the Human Race is for the completion of God's Purpose. The Human Race is the God Process *par excellence*. The Human Race exists for a purpose which is not Its own and which has always been viewed as a mystery.

Through Divine Revelation we come to realise the nature of Reality. The Godhead seeks to express Itself as a Collective Consciousness. In order to do this the Godhead must undergo the Process which has certain stages of development or evolution. The penultimate stage of this Process involves the Ultimate Ancestor *assuming* Human form, the Ultimate Ancestor *incarnating* for the purpose of Reproduction.

The Human Race has not been left 'in the dark' for the Godhead illuminates the path that Human beings are destined to travel. At crucial stages in the evolution of Human Culture, which will culminate in the appearance of the pre-destined Kingdom of God on Earth, Humanity receives further Revelation.

The Human Race has never been abandoned. The Human Race exists as the expression of the Predisposition of God to be God. We share a common history with all life and from the animal kingdom from which we may not claim exclusion. The Human Race is a pathway through the *relative unconsciousness* of Nature. The Human Race is an exodus from the past.

The Human Race is the key to the attainment of the Divine Identity which can realise Divine Destiny. The predisposed Life force through undergoing the Human Experience is channelled thereby towards the Realisation of Destiny. Guidance has always been there for the Human Race.

The Destiny of God is bound up with the Human Race; the Necessity of Human Nature is to express Predisposition. The Human Race is the *potential* Will of God.

The failure to understand the Mind of God renders a person incapable of evolving further; such a person is incapable of expressing the will of God. Such a person cannot jump 'the waterfall of Consciousness' *required* of those who will enter the Kingdom. Such a person, in failing the test, so to speak, will be as a guilty person, without excuse and without atonement.

The Unlimited, the Infinity of Space and of Consciousness, was *unconsciously* produced by means of the Predisposition of God to be God. *The Limit*, although it emanates from *The Unlimited*, is the growth of Consciousness, the possibility of purposeful behaviour. The Human Race, as *The Limit* and, within which there is potentially *no* limit in terms of Consciousness, is able to manifest Itself as the Consciousness of Predisposition.

We have the assurance that God is everything for there is nothing which is not God. We will be guided onwards and upwards to a Kingdom of God which will be built upon respect for all life, with all life viewed as being *One*.

> *Remember the Sabbath Day, to keep it holy. Six days you shall labour thereby doing all your work; but the seventh day is the Sabbath of the Lord, your God; in it you shall not work whether you, or your son, or your daughter, your manservant or maidservant, or your cattle, or the stranger that is within your gates. For in six days the Lord made the heavens and the Earth, the seas and all that is in them, and rested on the seventh day; wherefore the Lord blessed the Sabbath, and hallowed it.*

Implicit in the exhortation to *observe* the Sabbath there is the promise of the Sabbath being a *foretaste* of a Greater Life for the Human Race; this is a life which is the direct consequence of the Human Race overcoming *the curse* of having to work the Earth.

There is the promise that Humanity can surrender to the will of God, that the Human Race can put its trust in God as the Author of *all* Circumstances and, thereby, enter into the rest which is the *purpose* of the Sabbath.

It is of fundamental importance to people that they experience *a meaningfulness* in their lives. People need to believe that their efforts are of value, not only to themselves but to others. In addition to this it is psychologically and emotionally advantageous for people to believe that their efforts will make a difference towards the creation of a better life.

We have to pay a Blood Tax to Nature for our survival. Work has to be done. In the doing of that which is necessary for survival people can find meaning, worth and a sense of belonging. The work may be difficult and it may be dangerous, especially in time of warfare, but by means of participation in what is required for the well-being of the clan or the nation people can earn respect.

The Sabbath and its observance should be recognised as being for the benefit of the Human Race. It reminds us that our existence is dependent upon God and that we exist for the purpose which God has *for us*. We exist to facilitate the outworking of the purpose of God. The Human Race exists as the foreshadow of a better life for God with the Human Race existing as the means of manifesting the Divine Attributes.

There is a very real need for us to live balanced lives. Certainly we need to satisfy our material and emotional requirements; the balance required in our lives is in connection with the realisation that we have to sacrifice self-interest for a Greater Goal which will culminate in the Human Race entering the Sabbath.

Our existence on Earth must be an orderly one if we are to live in accordance with the promptings of an inner necessity to be creative. This involves the creation of circumstances for our further evolution, this being something that we do *intuitively*, or in accordance with Predisposition. No one exists in isolation. Our innermost selves are aware of the fact that we are all extensions of the Ultimate Ancestor, the fount of all Life.

Only work or activity which is the product of an *inner* creative compulsion can have real meaning. Mechanised work is lifeless, fit only for a lifeless machine. As long as the machine-economy remains an end in itself, rather than as a means of freeing the intellect from the burden of mechanical labour, people will continue to be *enslaved* and communities will continue to be fundamentally disordered. Humanity will lack cohesion. The Human Race will be divided.

Our attitude to work and to the payment of our Blood Tax to Nature for survival must change; this is superior by far to the mere betterment of outward circumstances. The superiority rests on the fact that *no matter* what difficulties we may experience in life we can overcome by being *creative*. Our creativity is our awakening to our Divine Origin *within* us. With the expression of the God-given creativity which abides within us, ignorance and destructive tendencies will be replaced.

We must see ourselves as being on a pilgrimage through Space and Time. The Self-Knowledge we require is Knowledge that our sojourn here on Earth has happened to us as fundamental to the unfolding of God's Divine Mission.

In remembering the Sabbath day we are aware of there being a constant battle between self-assertion and duty to friends, family, employers, church or political party. The need is for harmony. The achievement of such harmony is worked out in the concrete circumstances of Space and Time.

We should do as was the case in the Samuel narratives from the Old Testament. We should minister unto God in the presence of the people rather than ministering unto the people in the presence of God (8). The great problem today is knowing the will of God for our lives. This requires Revelation.

Our true duty is to establish *The Kingdom of God* on Earth. Our true duty is towards the *Oneness* of the Human Race and *all* life.

We must make our existence an ordered one. This will set the stage for our further evolution. This will permit us to enter into rest, the aim of the Sabbath. Thereby the fullness of the Sabbath will be experienced in us and through us.

We should be faithful to our families, our friends and to our nation and, above all, to the establishment of the Kingdom of God on Earth; in so doing, we will be true to ourselves.

Here is a reminder from Marcus Aurelius who was both a Roman Emperor and a philosopher:

"If you wouldst know contentment, let thy deeds be few," said the sage. Better still, limit them strictly to such as are essential, and to such as in a social being reason demands, and as it demands. This brings the contentment that comes of doing a few things and doing them well. Most of what we say and do is not necessary, and its omission would save both time and trouble. At every step, therefore, a man should ask himself, "Is this one of the things that are superfluous?" Moreover, not idle actions only but even idle impressions ought to be suppressed; for then unnecessary action will not ensue (9).

Honour your father and mother; that your days may be long upon the land which the Lord your God gives you.

When we are instructed to honour others we are being called upon to show *respect* to others. This is of considerable importance because in so doing, at the very least, we are recognising that others have as much right to be here as we do.

For the Guru Nanak (10), the founder of *Sikhism*, respect was all-important. There are inequalities in life, whether we like it or not, but these inequalities do *not* serve as an excuse for not showing respect to *all* life. One man can be a Prince and set to inherit 'insuperable kingly opulences' whereas another man can be desperately poor, so poor that he does not have a shirt to wear. Yet, for Nanak, they are still able to respect each other. It is this respect for others which will lead to the overcoming of all obstacles on the road to progress and, eventually, to the establishing of the Kingdom of God on Earth.

Respect was the basic building block of the outlook of the Guru Nanak. Respect is the dividing line between someone who is civilised and someone who is not civilised. It is such respect that renders Civilisation possible, indeed Civilisation is not possible without people who respect the feelings of others, as well as their beliefs and their property.

This respect should begin at home with the family because we are not alone and we don't come from nowhere. For some this will come across as a thorough over-simplification, especially when we consider that family life is not always satisfactory.

Before the author (John Houston) went to Glasgow University in 1977 employment was secured as a window cleaner. Some of the work entailed washing windows in hospitals and the author (John Houston) encountered people who were long-term residents, some having suffered terrible brain injuries because they had the misfortune of having drunken and violent fathers who beat them severely. Obviously, showing respect and honouring such parents and family could prove to be impossible. The author (John Houston) has met others who have confessed to hating their fathers.

On the other hand, years ago the author (John Houston) was speaking to a guest at a wedding reception. The man I was speaking to was wearing the kilt and, being intrigued, I asked him to identify the tartan he was wearing. In due course, he told me that it was a tartan pertaining to the Clan Gunn.

The man said that in wearing the kilt and displaying his tartan he was demonstrating that he didn't come from anywhere; furthermore, he wasn't alone. He had kinsmen and kinswomen all over the planet.

No one is able to go through life unaided. There is a whole framework already in operation to provide for the needs of the community. This includes orphans and other people who find themselves in an unwelcome state of isolation for they may have been deserted by others.

Under more acceptable conditions when a child comes into the world it comes into an *inheritance* which has been passed on for countless generations. We should honour inherited gifts. We recognise thereby that the growth of Human Civilisation has been progressing from immemorial Antiquity and, furthermore, we are custodians for our generation. We should honour and respect such an inheritance.

The foundation for Civilisation has already been laid. Each successive generation in inheriting the foundation can make it their very own in recognition of those who have gone before us, making the inheritance possible for those yet unborn.

As it is the will of God that the Kingdom of God should be established on Earth, *by* and *for* the purpose which God has for the Human Race we can readily appreciate that what has happened has been in accordance with the will of God. We should honour this.

Some will simply *perpetuate* the current Traditions which serve as a direct link to our Ancestors and, thereafter, to our Descendants. Others may be more inclined to Reformation or to Renewal to equip what should be a Living Tradition for changing circumstances. Whatever approach is adopted, we will have to discover *how* we comport ourselves as we face the future; none will be assured of success without the honouring of those who have gone before us because, as the majority of people are intent upon doing their best they, thereby, deserve our respect.

We can become immersed in the history of the clan or the nation. Yet the time will come, indeed the day will dawn, when we must step out of our past and go *beyond* Instruction.

Yet the future is *already* planned. We can do no more than what countless generations who have gone before us have done; they go *beyond* the instruction supplied by respected Ancestors, as is their duty, receiving guidance *directly* from the One who is 'the Beginning and End', as well as 'the First and the Last'.

We do not need to look for this Person for He will be revealed *to us*. This is a Promise from God, this promise being a supreme indicator of the respect that the Godhead has for us.

You shall not kill.

The *will* of God for the Human Race is that the Human Race lives according to Its nature; this is so because the Human Race has been created for a Purpose and for the fulfilment of that Purpose *of God*. For that Purpose to attain Its *predisposed* end, to which It aspires, the Human Race need do no more than live according to Its nature.

True Human activity is in terms of *Consciousness*. The Human Race is the manifestation of *how* Consciousness has evolved.

Still we come closer to that *Supreme Secret of the Ancients*, that Ancient Truth about the Human Race and *why* the Human Race exists.

The Evolution of the Human Race is the Evolution of the Consciousness *of* God. It is by means of the Human Race that the Ultimate Ancestor is able to manifest Itself as the Supreme Personality of Godhead. The Divine Attributes can be manifested by means of the Human Race, from whom the Supreme Personality of Godhead emerges, or *appears*.

The Divine Gnosis can be awakened by means of Humanity which is *predisposed* to recall its Divine Origin. This is the Result. This is the good end of the God Process.

Before this *pre-destined* state can be realised, however, the Human Race has to undergo an awakening. Ignorance must be replaced by Knowledge. This comes after a period of Instruction, this Instruction provided by a prophetic or philosophically-guided community, this Instruction assuming the form of a Religion. Thereby the coarseness of the uneducated can experience improvement.

The Western Philosophical tradition informs us that each one of us comes into the world *already equipped* to do something with excellence. This is in accordance with the will of God, with everything happening because of the so-called sovereignty of God, with life unfolding in accordance with the will of God, which can *never* be thwarted. It is therefore quite natural for people to be able to complement and supplement each other.

It is here that we should ponder a Truth about *Ourselves*; it is perfectly *natural* for people to be able to operate as a Collective Consciousness, as a Relationship of Godhead, within which the Supreme Personality of Godhead, from being One, is able to appear as 'the One amongst the Many'.

This brings us to the realisation that all *unnecessary* division, which is experienced as unnecessary competition, all vendettas, all rivalries which have their origin in jealousy, are ultimately *unnatural*. Being unnatural they are not part of God's greater aim and will therefore come to an end, everything which cannot *conform* to the outworking of the Purpose of God containing within itself the seeds of its own destruction.

All the unethical behaviour with which we are having to contend at this time has its origin in ignorance; the greatest ignorance of all is to be ignorant of the fact that *not only* are we potentially Divine but we are God in *disguise*; all our sorrows have their source in this ignorance. As has been the case from the

Ancient World, the truly civilised part of the Human community inescapably find themselves having to deal with people who are *uncivilised*.

Everything will culminate in the Day of Judgement when Human beings are divided into two separate groups: on the one hand, those who, because they are *suitable*, are able to enter the Kingdom; on the other hand, those who are unsuitable and, accordingly, have *no* future.

Those who are suitable know that it is wrong to take the life of another but they also recognise that, in dealing with those who are unsuitable and uncivilised, such people have to be taken in hand by those possessing power. If the uncivilised are left free to do what they are inclined to do in an *unrestricted* manner then they will create mayhem. Their behaviour will be unethical. They will have paid no heed to the consideration of others; neither will they have considered the effect of their actions upon the environment, their sole aim being their own selfish self-satisfaction.

When we look even closer at this 'inborn and irremediable division' which exists as the separation of Human beings into two distinct groups, we see that the *source* of this division is to be found in inclination or *intent*. The actions of a person are always coloured by their actual *intention*.

Here we recall words from the great *Moses Maimonides*; to the *wise* one word is sufficient. Those who are *wise* do not have to be told repeatedly that it is wrong to deliberately take a life. They know *intuitively* that such an act would be wrong and always regrettable. This is so even if subversives have to be eliminated, as the means of *displaying* to others that there is a level of behaviour which can *never ever be tolerated*.

The future belongs to those who are wise; in accordance with the Western Philosophical Tradition, the wise man or the wise woman is he or she who simply lives 'according to their nature', which is also the will of God for our lives.

It is natural for the Children of God to seek to express their true inclination; this will be their adherence to the will of God by means of which they become who they truly *are*.

The Children of God do not need to negotiate their way to uncovering their way through life; by the grace of god we can experience Divine guidance as a gift. This is the outworking of Destiny.

You shall not commit adultery.

There are many lessons to be learned as we journey through *Life*. For the author (John Houston) the most important lesson to learn is that *Life* has its own agenda. The importance of learning this is that we must *follow* that agenda. We exist for the unfolding of that Purpose.

From an early age I was to continually draw to my mother's attention that fact that I was convinced that I had lived before, the basis of this belief being no more than *intuition*. This was highlighted by the fact that when the Vision began to unfold it had become abundantly clear to me (John Houston) that the future had been planned out well in advance, with *nothing* left to Chance.

The Vision referred to something which *would happen* because the coming to pass of the Vision was pre-destined.

The Human Race exists for a Purpose, that Purpose being in connection with the pre-destined unfolding of *The Uncreated Vision* spoken of in the Hermetic Tradition. It is through following this Vision, through the apprehension of the Vision, that Humanity experiences Its Purpose in Life and this provides Life with *meaning*.

What the Law of Moses is drawing our attention to here is the need for *Faithfulness*. It is important for people to believe that they have been faithful in life; in being faithful they are exercising their intention of operating from a vantage point which is characterised by a sense of belonging.

The faithfulness alluded to here in the pronouncement, *You shall not commit adultery*, is a faithfulness which was intended to be life-long and exclusive, if need be. The faithfulness alluded to here is the faithfulness which makes possible the functioning of the Human community. It was no mere call to faithfulness within a monogamous relationship because, in the days of Moses, it was quite the custom to have more than one wife; having many wives was an indication of the blessing of Jehovah (11).

The attitude to the marriage relationship within the Biblical tradition is multi-faceted. Husbands and wives were expected to be faithful and, in addition to this, men were entitled to be polygamous; but those involved in the marriage relationship were, thereby, demonstrating that they were being faithful to Yahweh, the God of Israel.

There were exceptions to this however. In the return from the exile in Babylon at the time of Ezra and Nehemiah, men were encouraged to divorce wives who were of Babylonian heritage and whose approach to the worship of God was unacceptably syncretistic. The Cult of Yahweh was being polluted.

In the Old Testament Ezra was viewed as a *second Moses*. Ezra had been appointed to the position he occupied for the purpose of establishing the Law of Moses as the basis for the ordering of the life of the nation. Ezra was *as* a recollection of Moses. Ezra would provide the Jewish nation with a *bath-qol* (12), an *echo* of the original Moses. So great was the esteem in which Ezra was held that, in referring to Ezra, there was a custom to use the expression, "from Moses to Moses there was none greater than Moses (13)".

In *The Book of Ezra* we read:

> At length, Ezra the priest arose, and said to them: You yourselves have acted unfaithfully, in that you gave a dwelling to foreign wives so as to add to the guiltiness of Israel.
>
> And now make confession to Jehovah, the God of your forefathers and do his pleasure, and separate yourselves from the peoples of the land and from the foreign wives (14).

Within Israel there was such a thing as a *Levirite* marriage. This was permissible when a man died, for whatever reason, without issue. It was permissible for a brother or kinsman of the deceased man to provide the wife of the deceased with children, *on behalf* of the deceased. This was primarily for the sake of practicality. The important thing was that Yahweh be worshipped.

The warning that we should not commit adultery is a reminder that there is no profit in erring from a faithful life to God and to the nation.

The stance of the great Classical peoples to the marriage relationship was divergent. The Romans had a business-like view of marriage whilst the Greeks held a somewhat lofty conception.

> To the Roman citizen a house of his own and the blessing of children appeared the end and the essence of life. The death of the individual was not an evil, for it was a matter of necessity; but the extinction of a household or of a clan was injurious to the community itself, which in the earliest times therefore opened up to the childless the means of avoiding such a fatality by their adopting, in presence of the people, the children of others as their own (15).

In the Ancient World, as was the case with the Greeks, marriage was as much a public as it was a private affair. Rearing children within the family, as a forerunner to the children taking their place in the functions of the State, was viewed as both honourable and pleasant.

The marriage relationship provided a stability which would enhance the continuity of worshippers for the gods. This was earnestly taught to be necessary. The provision of *someone* to fulfil the children's office over one's own tomb was something sacred. Otherwise there was a serious risk of inherent difficulties in that other world 'beyond the grave'. This gave rise to the custom of adoption by childless couples.

You shall not steal.

As the Native Americans say, the man who *deliberately* takes the easy option in life will succeed only in weakening himself. Why should this be the case?

God, the Author of *all* circumstances, has decreed that it is correct for the Human Race to overcome the curse of having to work the Earth; it is therefore Divinely ordained that, through the best creative efforts of the Human Race, we create the circumstances for our own ascent to eventual assimilation into the Greater Life of God. In so doing, the Human Race is simply activating the Divine Predisposition for the sake of the expression of which, we exist.

For a successful life there is *no* substitute for creativity. For a successful life a person must have some initiative, some ability, some determination and ambition to see a project brought to completion and then, if need be, make alterations for greater efficiency and corresponding success.

We all come into the world *already equipped* to do something with excellence; this is something which Human beings can do, quite naturally, in service to others. Thereby with everyone doing that for which Nature, or God, has equipped them people can complement and supplement each other to operate more efficiently as a Collective Consciousness. Our task is to operate as One, although we are Many.

To do anything other than to operate in accordance with our Predisposition is to fail to operate in accordance with the purpose of living a truly Human life. A truly Human life can only be lived within the State, with the State existing to provide practical solutions to problems such as the rearing of children and the satisfaction of our material requirements. Communal activity is required for a civilised life.

The problem today is that there are so many people who are not living their lives in service to the State. Humanity is now having to come to terms with the fact that there are too many who have not had the benefit of a proper education. The resolution to this problem of defective education is the supply of education which is not defective.

Those who have had a proper education will realise their need to serve; they will see the need for the true purpose of education and, therefore, of Religion which is to render devotional service to others.

What people need to realise is that the Human Race is One and, accordingly, the suffering of each one of us is also, at the same time, the suffering of all. By the same token when someone enjoys success we can all benefit from this since life is for sharing.

You shall not bear false witness against your neighbour.

With the unfolding of the Divine Mind there is not and never can be an *ulterior* motive. Those who have an ulterior motive or who are found to have a hidden agenda are not doing the will of God.

What therefore is the true motive? The true motive of the Godhead is the Self-Realisation of the Predisposition of God to *be* God. This demands the Acquisition of an Identity, as a Collective Consciousness, which will be conducive to the Manifestation of the Absolute Glory of the Ultimate Ancestor, *as* the Supreme Personality of Godhead.

When the Predisposition of God is able to experience Self-Transcendence then such Predisposition has reached the Eternal State, thereby empowered to exist on an endless basis.

Needless to say that level of existence is still far removed from us. Humanity is still having to contend with petty-mindedness; indeed it would be true to say that petty-mindedness is the greatest enemy of the Human Race.

It is such petty-mindedness which always makes a point of sowing the seeds of discord. Behind this petty-mindedness there is the lurking problem of jealousy. Nothing can be gained from operating from the perspective of jealousy. To participate in activity founded on jealousy is to drink from a poisoned chalice. At the very least such behaviour is life-threatening for everyone who samples it.

The true cause for the jealousy is never mentioned. This is so because the perpetrator of the deed brought about by jealousy is actually in denial. An excuse for an altercation brought about by jealousy is never anything more than that, a mere excuse, a sop. The actual reason is not mentioned, far less acknowledged.

The jealous person is often depicted as doing what they consider to be correct because of dislike of another person. This is an illusion. People who operate from jealousy don't actually hate someone else at all; it is *themselves* that they hate. Seeing someone doing things, enjoying experiences or else attaining a status which the jealous person cannot, triggers self-loathing and it is this self-loathing which is the problem.

This calls for a review of *how* we interpret events. In the future when we encounter someone operating through jealousy doing, nonetheless, what they feel *compelled* and *justified* in doing, we must be able to identify the true cause of unwelcome discord. We must recognise that the motivation is *not* dislike of *another* person at all. The reason is actually low self-esteem.

People with low self-esteem will be unable to achieve much. They are hampered by the belief that other people are better than they are, although they may not admit this to themselves. People with low self-esteem expect that other people will have no interest in what they do or say. Bearing false witness is simply a means of attracting attention to themselves, *as victims*.

Such people are therefore doomed. They will never be able to experience the awakening of the Godhead within, they will never be able to encounter the Vision of a better life, a united Humanity within whose communities everything is done in accordance with the will of God. Unfortunately for them, they cannot see themselves depicted in such a scenario. Intuitively and *within themselves* they know that they do not belong there. The Kingdom of God is not for victims but for *overcomers*.

> *You shall not covet your neighbour's house, nor shall you covet your neighbour's wife, nor his manservant, nor his maidservant, nor his ox, nor his ass, nor anything that is your neighbour's.*

There is no greater mistake than to think that for happiness to be possible the only requirement is the possession of those things which, as is evident, already belong to other people in the community. Such material possessions feature strongly in the Media. It is often difficult to avoid them. They figure prominently in powerful propaganda from the Mass Merchandisers.

From the New Testament we have the exhortation from Jesus of Nazareth that "we should seek first the Kingdom of God and God's righteousness"; thereafter, what we truly require in life, will come *to* us. There is a Divine Provision. Thereby we are further equipped to accomplish the Divine Mission of the Human Race.

This demands the most thorough examination of our motives. Happiness in life does not necessarily come from the bettering of our circumstances but from a *change* of attitude towards our work and how we live our lives in general.

People seek freedom. They want to be able to enjoy the freedom of self-expression. They want to be free to be who they truly believe they should be. How unfortunate it is, however, that recognition of who we should be demands Wisdom, which is obviously *lacking* if someone is still searching for a most fundamental understanding pertaining to Self. The coming of the Word of God makes the difference.

Get-rich-quick-schemes, which should be avoided, exist in the world of popular Religion. On a number of occasions the author (John Houston) has listened to people speaking from the pulpit, proclaiming the existence of a God 'who takes requests', as though God were there primarily for *us*, for the satisfaction of our material needs.

The Creator God of old does not exist. The purpose of life is that God, as *Divine Identity*, be created. The Original Godhead, the Ultimate Ancestor of All, requires the Human Race as *the* means of the Creation of the Divine Identity. The Evolution of Godhead involves a stage whereby the Ultimate Ancestor, through *assuming* Human form is able to *reproduce* Itself by means of the Human Race.

Satisfaction can only be found through living a *purposeful* life; the one who lives a purposeful life is the one who is living according to one's *natural inclination*, or one's nature. The person who lives a purposeful life is the one who has realised that one's life is *not* one's own but that we belong to God.

When the Word of God comes to someone it is *no* Abstraction; the Word of God comes for the purpose of calling someone to action, to *do* the will of God, *not* our own selfish petty-minded will.

Through living according to our nature, which is in *compliance* with the unfolding of the purpose of God in the Acquisition of Identity, we will come into contact with like-minded people. There is nothing to compare with enjoying the fellowship of people who share a similar outlook.

When the author (John Houston) first made contact with Andrew James Collingwood, which was by telephone in July 1986, Ilbert (as he was called by friends) described himself as someone who characteristically 'collected people'. What a joy to be able to meet with other mystics!

People need the company of those who will bring out the best in them. Together they can operate from the vantage point of rendering devotional service. This makes true companionship possible. Through a Common Purpose they will delight in operating as One. They then witness the True Religion in action.

> *And all the people saw the thunderings and the lightnings, and the noise of the trumpet, and the mountain smoking; and when the people saw it, they removed and stood afar off. And they said unto Moses; speak with us and we will hear; but let not God speak with us, lest we die.*

Undeniably what we are witness to here is that there is a natural order in life and that this natural order is characteristically *hierarchical*.

Everywhere we look we are able to experience difference but we *never* see equality, even although we know what equality is. Equality *per se* does not exist because equality is *unnatural*. In life, however, because we seek to be civilised we should ensure that there should be equality of *opportunity*.

Nothing and no one should be permitted to undermine the ability of someone in the community to have access to education and to be enabled to contribute to the community through the rendering of devotional service. In the rendering of such devotional service, people contribute to the community by means of expressing the ability which has come *naturally*, for we are *predisposed*.

Because we are predisposed we can, therefore, *recognise* what is either advantageous or detrimental; our predisposition informs us *intuitively* what course of action we should take in life.

Moses is different from others in the community. Moses is the full expression of that Human Idea which others are not; in comparison, others are limited and imperfect sharings of the Idea which Moses brings *fully* to life. The essential Idea is the same, the difference being through Particulars.

When considering the Jesus of the New Testament, Rudolf Bultmann tells us that:

> Now, I think we can say that in the New Testament at least *parte potiori*, the pronouncements about Jesus' divinity or deity are not, in fact, pronouncements of his nature, but seek to give expression to his significance (16).

The implication here is that the Christ, the Son of God, introduced to us through the Western Philosophical Tradition, has been endowed with a nature which is essentially the same as our own. The Christ imparts his nature to us in as much as we *emanate* from this Son of God. We are *who* we *are* because of our Ultimate Ancestor who is actually fashioning us in the image of the Divine Archetype.

From Ancient times it was accepted among people that *receiving* the oracle of God was possible but it pertained only to a specific or select person, caste or clan; it is this very thing which we are witnessing in the Law of Moses as handed down to the Children of God *through* the prophet Moses.

Moses existed for this; all the training Moses had had in life was for the undertaking of this purpose. Moses had to be virtuous enough to be able to look upon the face of God and *not only* survive but receive Divine Revelation for the benefit of the entire community of faith.

As we stand at the crossroads of Destiny for the Human Race we must now anticipate the advent of a twenty-first century equivalent of the Biblical Moses; this twenty-first century Moses will be synonymous with a twenty-first century Hermes Trismegistus or a twenty-first century Thoth of the ibis beak.

How would we recognise Him? He will be physically attractive to an *unlimited* degree. He will have a countenance of *perfect beauty*; and there is more for his musical ability is unsurpassed thereby enabling him to reveal the *will* of God to the Human Race by means of Music. His instrument will be *the four-stringed lyre*.

Moses, Hermes or Ion, the Son of Apollo will speak to us in the language of God, which is Music. He will be beyond comparison as He unlocks the key to the Destiny of the Human Race. We will witness *for ourselves* and *through* Him the unfolding of the Divine Predisposition to be God.

NOTES

(1) The term *God Process* comes from the Rynachulaig years, as they are called.

In 1986 the author (John Houston) was first invited to the farm, known as Rynachulaig, in mid-Pershire. This was the opening gambit in a friendship which would last until 1999, ending with the death of my friend and mentor, Andrew James Collingwood. Among his friends he was referred to as *Ilbert*, a name he received from his days in Subud.

We had originally referred to life as *The Process of It*. The importance of *It* was paramount. *It* was everything with everything being, somehow or other, the *expression* of It.

What had fascinated Ilbert from an early age was that, as the Process of It unfolds, for the sake of that unfolding It had sought to express Itself as certain *types*.

This is nothing new for there are types in Psychology as well as in Astrology. These types existed for the sake of the Self-expression of It.

It was the author (John Houston) who coined the term *The God Process* and that the reason why these types were possible was because they existed as the expression of Predisposition. All life is predisposed. God, or It, if you prefer, is Predisposition, Itself.

The many long conversations we had, often in the company of others, played an inestimably important part in the appearance of the philosophy of John Houston.

(2) Giles Sparrow, *Cosmos: A Field Guide*. Published by *Quercus*. From the cover.

> A few hundred years ago we believed the Universe was bound by a crystal sphere speckled with fixed Stars. Less than a century ago, we believed the Milky Way to be its entire extent. Now we know it stretches at least 130 billion trillion kilometres (80 billion trillion miles) in every direction around us. We know that the magnificent vault of Stars emblazoning Earth's night skies are an infinitesimal fraction of the hundreds of billions that inhabit our Galaxy, and we know that there are at least as many Galaxies in the Universe as there are Stars in the Milky Way. We know that our Galaxy is a member of a cluster of Galaxies that is itself an out-lying member of a super cluster 100 million light years across, but which is a part of a filament that stretches a billion light years across Space.

Giles Sparrow states 'the Big Bang' was an event which happened 13.7 billion years ago, by means of which the Universe exploded into existence and started to expand.

The author (John Houston) is of the opinion that it is *incorrect* to assert that the Origin of the Universe was in what we refer to as 'the Big Bang'. It should be recognised that 'the Big Bang' was *not* the Beginning that 'once was'.

'The Big Bang' was the *initial effect* of the Predisposition of God to be or to become God. In this context, 'the Big Bang' was the inauguration of a Biological Process, a Process of *Personalisation*, the aim of which was to provide an Identity for the Ultimate Ancestor who is *predisposed to exist*.

Prior to 'the Big Bang' there was only Predisposition; this Predisposition to *be* God, in experiencing Itself as the Archetype, became the Ultimate Ancestor of All when, in accelerating to the speed of light, which It was predisposed to do, It acquired apparently Infinite Possibility.

For the author (John Houston) what is so amazing about all of this is that from a speck of Matter, weighing 10^{-50} grammes, measuring 10^{-33} centimetres, and from a Process lasting all of 10^{-30} seconds, *these being approximations*, 13.7 billion years later we are considering this Process and *how* it could possibly relate to us.

(3)   Peter Dawkins, *Arcadia. Studies in Ancient Wisdom*. Published by *The Francis Bacon Research Trust* in 1988, page 61.

This refers to Initiation into the penultimate stage of *The Greater Mysteries of Egypt*.

The candidate took his new oath and the history of the gods was explained to him, including how they emanate from the One Sole God.

After the reception the new MAAWR was led up from the crypt and into a great hall via the Gate of the Gods. Here he saw the pantheon of the gods represented and identified in order, and their meanings explained. The more esoteric nature of the history of Egypt, the World, the Universe and of the Society and is Its Order, was then taught to him by the Demiourgos. He was given a list of all the Chief Inspectors of the Society, past and present, and a table of the members of the Society throughout the World.

The word of the degree was *ibis*. The work of the degree was to become proficient in Astrology. Finally he was taught the Priestly Dance.

(4)   The revelation of the Human Race as God incarnate came slowly; indeed this Truth was not revealed to those who were considered unworthy. People had to be prepared for this Knowledge. Nonetheless, True Religion is a *relative* term.

From the time of the Gnostics especially, when people started to meet in large population centres which existed due to the Roman Empire, the old *national* forms of Religion went into decline. People were looking for something better, something that would provide people with *further* Divine Revelation.

From their standpoint the True Religion was a Religion embracing all Religions, a Religion which would provide a Gnosis about the Origin and Destiny of the Human Race. Many felt that this had been achieved by *The Cult of Jesus Christ* whereas, later, others would put their faith in the prophet Muhammed.

What can the term True Religion mean for us today?

It means the Truth about the Human Race and why the Human Race exists. The True Religion pertains to Knowledge rather than to mere belief. The Knowledge it imparts comes as Recollection.

The True Religion, furthermore, recognises that the purpose of Religion is to *educate* the population in a systematic manner. The purpose of the True Religion is to lay the foundations of a Human Civilisation, Religion existing to *civilise* people, to teach people respect for others because we are as *One*.

The True Religion is Humanity united under the sovereign Lordship of the Supreme Personality of Godhead for the establishment of a Kingdom which will last 'until times indefinite'.

All those whom we recognise as Prophets, such as Krishna or Apollo, the Buddha Gautama, Mahavira, Plato, the Jesus of the New Testament, the prophet Muhammed, the guru Nanak and so on, *all* proclaimed a message which had three essential elements.

For us today *all* authentic Religions proclaim the Oneness of the Human Race, indeed *all* life. There is also the recognition of *non-violence* as the foundation of all Human interaction. Then there were the fundamentals of moral rectitude.

The True Religion is the means for the realisation of Destiny for the Human Race; the True Religion brings people together for the *purpose* of the Realisation of Destiny.

This involves the Realisation that the Human Race *is* Divine and that the True Identity of the Human Race is the Godhead, a Collective Consciousness, as has been hinted at in Hinduism with Brahma, Visnu and Shiva or with the Father, Son and Holy Ghost from the Biblical Revelation.

Not all Humans will be able to inherit the Kingdom and even fewer will be able to cross-fertilise with those from the world of the Biblical Angels. Only the fruit of the Human Race will be able to experience *complete* assimilation into the Greater Life of God as expressed by the Galactic Confederation of Humanities.

The True Religion recognises the appearance of and the deifying of the Human Race as *the work* of God with the Godhead predisposed to even greater Self-Realisation on higher levels of Consciousness.

(5) *The Dialogues of Plato*. Translated by Benjamin Jowett. Published by *The Encyclopaedia Britannica, Inc*, in Chicago, 1996 edition, page 76

From *The Euthydemus* of Plato we read those words of Socrates which state that "Knowledge of some kind is the only good".

(6) As above. Page 67.

In *The Euthydemus of Plato* we read of Socrates saying, "then after all the wise are the learners and not the unlearned".

(7) *The Acts of the Apostles*, chapter 17, verses 28-29.

(8) In the late 1970s the author (John Houston) attended a series of Bible studies at a Church of Scotland in Glasgow. The minister was a Reverend Sutherland and we studied the Samuel narratives from the Old Testament.

Reverend Sutherland taught that from the Samuel narratives it was possible to discern that success in the spiritual life is to be found in ministering to *God* in the presence of the people.

The Reverend Sutherland maintained that the Church was making a quite fundamental error because rather than ministering unto God in the presence of the people we were mistakenly ministering *unto people* in the presence of God.

(9) Marcus Aurelius Antoninus, *Meditations*. With an Introduction by Maxwell Staniforth and a Preface by A.C Grayling. Published by *The Folio Society* in 2002 (MMII). See Book IV, verse 24.

Marcus Aurelius Antoninus lived from 121 to 180 AD.

(10) The Guru Nanak lived from 1469 until 1539. He was born in Lahore which is now part of Pakistan.

He was raised as a Hindu. He travelled widely among both Hindu and Muslim communities teaching spiritual truth.

He settled in Kartarpur in the Punjab where he began to attract followers. His Doctrine, which was set out in a systematic manner in *The Adi-Granth*, sought a fusion of Brahmanism and Islam on the grounds that both were monotheistic.

It had been claimed that his own personal beliefs were characteristically polytheistic.

(11) *The Second Book Of Samuel*, Chapter 12, 7-8

(12) The literal translation of 'bath-qol' is 'daughter of voice'.

(13) There is a divergence of opinion among Old Testament scholars in connection with the chronology of *The Book of Ezra* and *The Book of Nehemiah*.

Some say that Nehemiah predates Ezra but Ezra is portrayed as earlier than Nehemiah because of the importance attributed to Ezra, as the *Second Moses*.

As was the case with *The Book of Daniel*, *The Book of Ezra* was written partly in Hebrew and partly in Chaldee.

The Chaldee begins at the eighth verse of the fourth chapter, continuing to the end of the eighteenth verse of the sixth chapter. The Chaldee reappears in chapter seven, verse twelve to twenty-six.

(14) *The Book of Ezra*, Chapter 10 v 10f.

(15) Theodor Mommsen, *A History of Rome. From the Foundation of the City to the Sole Rule of Julius Caesar*. Translated by W.P Dickson. Introduced by Anthony Grafton. Edited by C.J Shepherd. Published by *The Folio Society*, London in 2006 (MMVI). From the second chapter, *The Original Constitution of Rome*, page 17.

(16) Rudolf Bultmann, *Philosophical Essays*. Published by SCM Press, London in 1955. Page 280.

18: Towards Transcendence

I

It is of considerable importance to those alive today to realise that for the best part of two millennia, those whose Ancestors had lived in 'the known world' under Roman rule had been subjected to a Royal Lie.

The *purpose* of the Royal Lie was to give to the uneducated something, indeed *Someone*, to believe in. The true notion concerning God was deliberately withheld from the uneducated mass of the population. The Royal Lie propagated by the Vatican was known as *The Gospel of Jesus Christ*; the Vatican *indoctrinated* people to believe that they were *fallen*, being tainted with Original Sin (1).

The Royal Lie was well-intentioned (2). The purpose of the Royal Lie was Law-enforcement by means of Superstition, or supernatural Law-enforcement, if you prefer. It was the only education people would receive, the true purpose of such education being preparation for citizenship.

Now with the Christian and Islamic Eras both concluded and Humanity in the cusp between two Ages, we can expect *The Cult of Jesus Christ* and Islam, its Eastern counterpart, to be phased out by God. The Royal Lie is now more of a hindrance than an asset.

Here we ask the question: if *The Cult of Jesus Christ* and *Islam* are to be abandoned by God as rudimentary methods of preparing the Human Race for Initiation into the Western Philosophical Tradition what, or *who*, will act as their replacement?

There can only be one answer to this question and it is this: the Word of God must come to the Human Race. The Ultimate Ancestor must appear and, in being *recognised* intuitively as such, this Hermes, Krishna or Apollo will unite the Earth under His rule. Thereafter He will fashion the future Human Race in His own image.

It has been through the medium of the Human Race that the Ultimate Ancestor has increasingly activated Its Internal Potency; through following the Vision of Its own Self-Realisation, Knowledge gained from this experience comes *as* Recollection.

Additionally, through the medium of the Human Race, the Ultimate Ancestor will be empowered to Remember Its Divine Origin, which is now *Reborn* as the Supreme Personality of Godhead.

The Supreme Personality of Godhead is now able to Reproduce. Here we have the beginnings of the next stage of our evolution; here we have the appearance of a new Humanity, born of a Quantum Leap in Consciousness, brought about by the Incarnation of the Ultimate Ancestor.

Thereafter the Earth will witness the advent of a new and *more deified* Humanity which is now much more equipped to manifest the Perfect Proportion of the Divine Archetype. This must surely be what Lord Krishna referred to when He informs us that "in every millennium He will be made manifest in His Original Transcendental form" (3).

This Recollection of the Divine Origin of all alters everything. The Destiny of the Human Race and indeed, thereby, the Destiny of the Godhead is *dependent* upon the Human Race being able to Remember that Predisposed Impulse which brought everything to life.

The Creation of God as a Self-evolving Being (4) is for the purpose of expressing the Predisposition of God to be God.

Now at the time of an Epochal Threshold, things must now alter quite dramatically because this Process of the Evolution of Consciousness is actually *non*-linear (5).

We are set to undergo a 'mass-extinction event'. The Human Race cannot turn back the clock. Too much or too little water, the advent of famine, the spread of disease and warfare will see millions of people wiped out. This 'mass extinction event from within' by what is 'the self-controlled system of life on Earth' will create a new kind of world for us.

The Western Philosophical Tradition recognises Knowledge as Recollection. The purpose of the Human Race is to provide God with a means of Recollection. The Incarnation of the Ultimate Ancestor is for the purpose of Recollection. By means of Remembering the Divine Origin, the Ultimate Ancestor can become the Supreme Personality of Godhead, then reproduce to *further* deify Humanity.

II

In *The Meno* of Plato we are confronted with a remarkable conversation pertaining to the Acquisition of Knowledge. In previous chapters we have seen how this Holy Knowledge (Gnosis) comes *as* Recollection.

The conversation develops as follows:

Meno: And I am certain that no one ever did teach him!

Socrates: And yet he has the knowledge.

Meno: The fact, Socrates, is undeniable.

Socrates: But if he did not acquire the knowledge in this life, then he must have learned it at some other time.

Meno: Clearly he must.

Socrates: Which must have been the time when he was *not* a man.

Meno: Yes!

Socrates: And if there have always been true thoughts in him, both at the time when he *was* and *was not* a man, which only need to be awakened into knowledge by putting questions to him, the soul must always have possessed this knowledge, for he always either was or was not a man.

Meno: Obviously!

Socrates: And if the truth of all things always existed in the soul, then the soul is immortal.

In addition to this, in *The Phaedo*, we read something similar.

> Cebes added: "Your favourite doctrine, Socrates, that knowledge is recollection, *if* true, also necessarily implies a previous time in which we have learned that which we now recollect. But this would be impossible *unless* our soul had been in some place before existing in the form of Man."

As the evolution of the God Process *naturally* unfolds there has been the necessity of the ability to *assume* Human form. It is by means of the Human Race that the pre-destined Recollection of the Divine Origin is possible. The evolution of the Human Race is the evolution of the Inclination, expressed as *Humanity*, of being able to render such Recollection possible.

True Human activity is in terms of the evolution of Consciousness, with the One possessing such Knowledge being *already* Divine. The One who possesses such Knowledge is a *new kind* of Human being; this is a Humanity which is equipped for life into the future and to the *Realisation* of Destiny.

If the Human Race can produce a Recollection of the Divine Origin then the Human Race will be equipped to serve as *a means* of Existence; the Human Race is thereby able to furnish the requirements of a Predisposed Life-Force which *uses* the Human Race for the outworking of the Divine Purpose.

The Process of Evolution, which is also the *unfolding* of the God Process, is the *Preparation* of the Human Race as the means *of* Existence for the Godhead and on an on-going basis.

The Supreme Personality of Godhead *is the Awakening* of the Divine Essence of the Human Race, the further Awakening of the Predisposition to be God.

With the greater Awakening of the Predisposition to be God by means of the Human Race, a new Humanity appears. These will be Human beings who are the Realisation of the Divine Predisposition to create a Collective Consciousness which will overcome the curse of life as we know it, with its inevitable decay and death. Such a Humanity would have to be Self-evolving.

The Human Race is, therefore, in preparation for the arrival of the One whose *Earthly* manifestation is *as* Hermes Trismegistus. The Growth of Complexity in Nature is for the purpose of creating a means of Transcendence for the One who is made manifest as Hermes Trismegistus, as Krishna or as

Ion, the Son of Apollo. The Godhead must express Itself, being *predisposed* to exist.

The Ultimate Ancestor, *as* the Expression of the Predisposition of God to be God, being predisposed to exist *will*, therefore exist *no* matter what.

God will exist. In life, this is the only certainty. God *will* exist and so will *we*, to enable the manifestation of the Ultimate Ancestor as the Supreme Personality of Godhead. This is the outworking of the Predisposition *of* God to *be* God (6). It happens in beehives and anthills everywhere.

The Godhead must create a means of Self-expression for Predisposition. This is the *Uncovering* of an Idea, *not* the Discovery of an Idea. Here we remember that Plato's *Theory of Ideas* has as its basis that Knowledge *originates* in Ideas. The expression of an Idea requires Form; the expression of the Idea whose Predisposition is to be or to become God, requires the Human Race, which embodies the Divine Attributes.

The Platonic Theory can be summed up by saying that the Mind thinks and knows by means of Genera and Species which, according to Plato, are actually *Ideas*.

The Divine Memory must be awakened. The Racial Memory of the Ultimate Ancestor is the Human Race. This Ultimate Ancestor is the One who appears to us as Hermes Trismegistus or Krishna or Apollo.

Life is expressed by means of Containment. The evolution of the Universe has produced the Human Race, by means of whom the Unfolding of the Predisposition of God to be God is rendered possible.

By means of the Human Race Self-Transcendence can be attained, the Human Race existing as the means for the Recollection of the Divine Origin of life. The Awakening of Apollo is the Awakening of the Divine Humanity.

The Human Race facilitates the Rebirth of the Mind. The Human Race is the entrance to the Divine Mind; the Human Race exists as *the* means of God to experience Destiny. The Recollection of the Divine Origin brings that Divine Origin to life. The Divine Origin, the Ultimate Ancestor, has been Reborn by means of the Human Race.

By means of the Human Race the Ultimate Ancestor can realise Destiny. The Ultimate Ancestor, by means of Humanity, can experience Its Destiny of being able to live as a Collective Consciousness on an endless basis.

The Old Humanity which lived and then died but which was incapable of expressing *satisfactorily* the Divine Predisposition to be God will come to an end; in its place a new and Reborn Humanity will appear. This New Humanity is equipped to guide the Godhead to the Realisation of Destiny.

The Human Race exists *as* the Expression of the Original Idea. This Idea is *predisposed* to create an Identity which will permit the Self-expression of the Predisposition which the Idea *represents*. By means of Time, *as* Process, the Idea unfolds to live in accordance with Its nature.

The evolution of the Human Race is also the evolution of the Ultimate Ancestor. The evolution of the Human Race will lead to the appearance of Hermes Trismegistus, or Krishna or Ion, the Son of Apollo.

With the Incarnation of Hermes, *The Messenger of gods*, the Human stage of our evolution will have been completed.

It is by means of the Human Race that Hermes is able to evolve. The Incarnation of Hermes as a Human being enables Hermes to reproduce; this is an evolutionary leap for Hermes as well as for the Human Race. Humanity is now more Divine. Each Human reproduced by Hermes is a potential Hermes. Unlike the Old Humanity the New Humanity is equipped to experience Divinity.

The appearance of Hermes, or Krishna or Apollo is the Activation of the Racial Memory of the Ultimate Ancestor, which is the Human Race.

The Destiny of the Godhead is *dependent* upon the Awakening of the Racial Memory of the Ultimate Ancestor, which is the Human Race.

Once this Rebirth has taken place, there will be the appearance of a new generation of Human beings who are descended from the One who has taken a Quantum Leap in Consciousness. This draws to our attention that since this Rebirth is *only* for those who have descended from Hermes, the Human Race is inescapably divided into two distinct groups.

There is *only* Predisposition whose Self-expression is *as* Existence. That Predisposition will instinctively create the circumstances for Its own Appearance.

It seeks to reproduce Itself as a Collective Consciousness enabling It to relate to Itself as It, and *only* It, actually exists.

It activates Its Racial Memory, which is Humanity. Divinity is therefore possible.

A new Humanity appears for the next stage of evolution. The Evolutionary Process culminates in the Full Recollection of the Ultimate Ancestor.

The Human Race is the Identity for the Racial Memory of the Ultimate Ancestor. The Total Realisation of all the Humanities will be the Total Recall of our Ultimate Ancestor.

III

It is sometimes easy to become so seduced by the elevated language of much of the Ancient Wisdom that we tend to forget that the purpose of life is about the unfolding of the Divine Identity of a Person, and a Person with a task to fulfil.

It is about the Appearance of a Person who has come to Earth to rule. He has a peculiar function to perform. He must explain who He is and what is the Purpose which He seeks to accomplish. He has Eternity in mind.

Here again we remember those words of Lord Krishna from *The Bhagavad-Gita*:

> Never was there a time when I did not exist, nor you, nor all these kings; nor in the future shall any of us cease to be.

The One who is the fount of the Pure Idea comes into Existence *predisposed* to create an environment conducive to the manifestation of the Pure Idea unto Infinite Complexity. The Recollection of the Divine Origin, or perhaps preferably, the Awakening of the Supreme Personality to that Recollection alters everything; nothing can ever be the same again.

The Ultimate Ancestor identifies Himself with that Predisposition which makes everything possible; thus in *The Bahagavad-Gita* we read:

> O son of Prtha, know that I am the original seed of all existences, the intelligence of intelligent, and the prowess of all powerful men (7).

Krishna continues:

> By Me, in My unmanifested form, this entire Universe is pervaded. All beings are in Me, but I am not in them. And yet everything that is created does not rest in Me. Behold My mystic opulence! Although I am the maintainer of all living entities and although I am everywhere, I am not a part of this cosmic manifestation, for My Self is the very source of all creation (8).

He continues further:

> I am the Supersoul, O Arjuna, seated in the hearts of all living entities. I am the beginning, the middle and the end of all beings (9). Furthermore, O Arjuna, I am the generating seed of all existences. There is no being, moving or non-moving, that can exist without Me (10).

Through the Activation of Its Racial Memory which is the Human Race, the Supreme Personality becomes the progenitor of a New Humanity sufficiently awake to know *their* predisposed Purpose.

They will also know that, as Racial Memory, the further unfolding of the Memory results in a more deified Humanity. This is a Humanity which exists to guide the Predisposed Life-force, which evolves as the Human Race, to Its Ultimate Destination.

Being the Key to the attainment of Divine Destiny, the Absolute can take another leap in Consciousness towards Its own Self-Realisation, by means of the Human Race, Its Racial Memory.

What does the Ultimate Ancestor, who is the Self-expression for the Divine Predisposition to be God, seek to achieve by His Incarnation? He tells us that:

> Whenever or wherever there is a decline in religious practice (11), O descendant of Bharata, and a predominant rise in irreligion, at that time I descend Myself (12).

The Supreme Personality of Godhead is predisposed to exist and *will* exist, thereafter, *no* matter what. What can the motive be for the Appearance of the One who is the fount of all Life? The One, the Ultimate Ancestor, seeks Self-expression as a Collective Consciousness, and on an endless basis.

The One is predisposed to follow a particular line of action because:

> Everyone is forced to act helplessly according to the qualities he has acquired from the modes of material nature; therefore no one can refrain from doing something, not even for a moment (13).

Krishna reveals that He is actually safeguarding the Destiny of the Human Race. This is something He does *as* the rendering devotional service.

> If I did not perform prescribed duties, all these worlds would be put to ruination. I would be the cause of creating unwanted population, and I would thereby destroy the peace of all living beings (14).

There is also the Purpose of Reproduction to further *deify* the Human Race. A new kind of Human being will then be possible. Such beings are reproduced by Krishna.

> The total material substance, called Brahman, is the source of birth, and it is that Brahman that I impregnate, making possible the births of all living beings, O son of Bharata (15).

Something from that "other world of the Biblical Angels" is now active within a Humanity which has world-wide Media. The One who is predisposed to exist as the Supreme Personality of Godhead will start to transform Humanity.

The One, to whom the Earth belongs as an inheritance, will continue to create a Human Race 'in His own image', as He is predisposed to do.

> By becoming fixed in this Knowledge, one can attain the transcendental nature like My own. Thus established, one is not born at the time of creation or disturbed at the time of dissolution (16).

There will be the dawning of a New Day, the establishing of a Kingdom which will last 'until times indefinite'. This Kingdom exists for the Appearance of and the Purpose of the Divine Pharaoh, to utilise Egyptian terminology.

This is the One who is predisposed to exist *as* the Human Race. *The Limit* and *The Unlimited*, being Modes of Action within the All, are united by means of Transcendence.

NOTES

(1)   The purpose of the Royal Lie was to render people psychologically dependent upon the Catholic Priesthood; for the Religion of Rome *only* the Catholic Priesthood could administer the Sacraments, thus ensuring forgiveness. Viewing themselves as successors to the Apostle Peter, they were portrayed as holding the Keys of the Kingdom.

     The Protestant Reformers saw things differently, of course. For the Protestant Reformers the salvation of the Human Race was not dependent upon the Catholic Priesthood at all because it was the gift of God.

     Protestantism recognises from Scripture that there is an elect group who God has chosen for participation in the future Kingdom. Salvation is *not* the outcome of people choosing to become Christians because, for the believer, there was *no* choice. The only people who would ultimately be saved were those whom God had chosen.

(2)   The propagation of the Gospel of Jesus Christ was well-intentioned. It was not the Whole Truth, so to speak; it was what the Vatican wanted people to believe.

     The Gospel which the Vatican created for Its own purposes was designed to inculcate Virtue among the uneducated. Its three major principles were: non-violence should characterise Human dealings and decision-making; the Gospel sought the recognition of the *Oneness* of the Human Race; there was the promotion of those fundamentals of moral rectitude.

(3)   His Divine Grace A.C. Bhaktivendata Swami Prabhupada, *The Bhagavad-Gita as It is*. Published by *The Bhaktivedanta Book Trust* in 2003. From the fourth chapter, entitled *Transcendental Knowledge*. See verse 6.

> Although I am unborn and My transcendental body never deteriorates, and although I am the Lord of all living entities, I still appear in every millennium in My original transcendental form.

(4) There is the requirement of the appearance of a Collective Consciousness. This is for the expression of the One who, by means of Form and by means of the Change, which Form permits, can manifest Itself as the Supreme Personality of Godhead.

There is *only* Predisposition whose Self-expression is *as* Existence. That Predisposition will instinctively create the circumstances for Its own Appearance. It seeks to reproduce Itself as a Collective Consciousness enabling It to relate to Itself as It, and *only* It, actually exists. It activates Its Racial Memory, which is the Human Race. Divinity is therefore possible, indeed *pre-destined*.

A new Humanity will appear as the next stage of our evolution. The Evolutionary Process culminates in the Full Recollection of the Ultimate Ancestor.

The Human Race, as Racial Memory, is the Identity of the Ultimate Ancestor who is the Original Godhead.

(5) The Evolutionary Process, which is also the God Process, expresses Itself as a progression which is *non-linear* in character.

The fact that the Process of Evolution is *non-linear* is brought about by the fact that there are no straight lines in Nature.

Evolution takes place by means of 'leaps' or 'jumps'. This is why no one now talks of 'the missing link'.

Among the so-called Celtic peoples, the salmon were revered because the salmon were able to return home without instruction. In Gaidhlig, salmon are referred to as *bradan*, pronounced bratan, from which the words *Britain* and *Briton* are derived as corruptions.

Quite apart from the fact that the salmon can return home without Philosophy, Politics and Religion is amazing enough in and of itself; as the salmon return home they will have to jump up waterfalls, to a higher level.

(6) His Divine Grace A.C. Bhaktivendanta Swami Prabhupada, *The Bhagavad-Gita as It is*. Published by *The Bhaktivedanta Book Trust* in 2003. From the second chapter entitled *Contents of the Gita Summarised*, Text 12, page 88.

Never was there a time when I did not exist, nor you, nor all these kings; nor in the future shall any of us cease to be.

(7) as (6) above. See Chapter 7.11.

(8) as (6) above. See Chapter 9.4 – 5.

(9) as (6) above. See Chapter 10.20

(10) as (6) above. See Chapter 10.39.

(11) The word *Religion* is often difficult to define since people are not readily aware that the purpose of Religion is to provide Instruction for people. This Instruction was preparation for citizenship, for the civilising of the Human Race. Religion encourages people to render devotional service and to show consideration to others. Religion seeks to unite people in a common purpose.

The word *Religion* comes via Old French from Latin, derived from the word *religare* which means 'to tie up'. It is a combination of *Re* plus *ligare* which means 'to bind together'.

(12) as (6) above. See Chapter 4.7.

(13) as (6) above. See Chapter 3.5.

(14) as (6) above. See Chapter 3.24.

(15) as (6) above. See Chapter 14.3.

(16) as (6) above. See Chapter 14.2.

19: The Divine Pharaoh

I

We have seen how life as we know it is only possible because of Predisposition which, being predisposed to exist, *will* exist *no* matter what. The Process of Evolution develops, quite naturally, as the unfolding of the Original or Pure Idea.

This is the Creation of a *means* of Existence, the Creation of an Identity for the Original Idea, the Original Idea being predisposed to exist as a Collective Consciousness and on an on-going basis.

The One, to whom the Earth belongs as an inheritance, will continue to deify the Human Race, thereby creating a Human Race 'in His own image' as per His requirements. The One seeks to *prepare* the Human Race, as the Evolution of Consciousness, to become His eternal abode.

In further deifying the Human Race, the Ultimate Ancestor takes another step towards Evolution attaining completion; the evolution of the Ultimate Ancestor is the evolution of 'the One amongst the Many'.

The Evolution of the Original Idea means that the Original Idea, when conceived by Predisposition Itself will, quite naturally, evolve towards the Full Transcendence of Predisposition.

The Original Idea was, is and always will be the Self-expression of the Predisposition to become 'the One amongst the Many'. The Original Idea involved the Self-expression of an Idea which requires to exist as a Relationship of Self (1), or as a Collective Consciousness.

The world and the Human Race as we know It, existing as they do within the context of the One evolving as 'the One amongst the Many', will inevitably reach an Omega point (2), the end of one stage and the beginning of another. A New Day will dawn. The Kingdom of God, apprehended within the dreams and visions of the Mystics and Prophets of all Ages, will make Its appearance, in accordance with the unfolding of Predisposition.

This Kingdom exists for the Appearance of and the Purpose of the newly-emerged Divine Pharaoh, to utilise Egyptian terminology. It will not end there because it will also prominently feature *the sacred ibis*, which is symbolic of the Egyptian god, Thoth of the ibis beak, whose task is the restoration of harmony (3).

This harmony, which *The Messenger of the gods* exists to establish on Earth, is purposeful indeed! First of all the Human Race must be united by means of a Common Purpose. This will be the laying, with the consent of the Human Race, of the foundation of a Kingdom which will exist 'until times indefinite'.

Thereafter, work will begin for the specific purpose of reducing the size of the Human population. As things stand, *over population* is the greatest problem confronting the Human Race, so much so that unless definite action is taken to deal with this problem, the Destiny of the Human Race is seriously threatened.

From the Hermetic Tradition, which was the undercurrent of the Western Philosophical Tradition we see that Zeus, fearing the entire destruction of the Human Race, sends Hermes to bring order to our cities; by the same token Lord Krishna renders devotional services to us by manifesting Himself for the purpose of *eliminating unwanted* population (4).

In 2008, specifically, there was a Press Release from the think-tank known as *The Optimum Population Trust*. Its message was stark. The Press Release stated that "the Earth can no longer support the number of people who live in it". If population were to continue to grow at present rates, it will end in wars and mass starvation.

Calling for greater care to be taken pertaining to the unacceptable level of the Human population is hardly a new thing.

In her 1922 book, *Pivot of Civilisation*, Sanger (5) thoroughly condemned charitable action. She devoted a full chapter to the denigration of charity and the deprecation of the lower classes. Chapter five, *The Cruelty of Charity*, was prefaced by an epigraph from Spencer (6) himself: fostering the good-for-nothing at the expense of the good is an extreme cruelty. It is a deliberate storing-up of miseries for future generations. There is no greater curse to posterity than that of bequeathing them an increasing population of imbeciles...

She condemned philanthropists and repeatedly referred to those needing help as little more than *human* waste. "Such philanthropy... unwittingly promotes precisely the results most deprecated. It encourages the healthier and more normal sections of the world to shoulder the burden of the unthinking and indiscriminate fecundity of others, which brings with it... a dead weight of human waste. Instead of decreasing and aiming to eliminate the stocks that are most detrimental to the future of the Race and of the world, it tends to render them to a menacing degree dominant (7)".

For Henry Fairfield Osborn (8) it all came down to one mandate: as Scientists have enlightened Governments in the prevention and spread of disease, they must also enlighten Governments to the need to prevent the multiplication of worthless members of Society.

Osborn was supportive of the standard Eugenic idea, which was, "the true spirit of American democracy that *all men are born with equal rights and duties* has been confused with the political sophistry that 'all men are born with equal character and ability to govern themselves'."

II

There is a Great Truth for us to recognise here: the whole of life is but the unfolding of the Original Idea. This is an Idea which is predisposed to exist and, therefore, will experience Existence *as* the unfolding of Self, in accordance with the Predisposition which *inclines* us to live according to our nature. This is what the author (John Houston) refers to as the God Process.

This God Process cannot be thwarted. There is a very real inevitability to the God Process. Being the fount of all life, the 'black hole' from which light shines on everything else, being the *cause* of Existence, has only Its own Destiny to pursue. Within this context, everything is predisposed; everything is predestined; everything is prearranged.

The most liberating experience in life is when we realise that there is actually no choice and that there is something better; there is the promise from God that we can and will be able to live according to our nature, thereby exemplifying our Divine Attributes.

Those with prophetic insight recognise intuitively that there is a Divine Plan and that it is *already* in action. It cannot be stopped.

From the New Testament we read of how the primitive Christian community had come into existence and was growing in size and influence. Then there was a backlash:

> But the High Priest and all those with him, the then existing sect of the Sadducees, rose and became filled with jealousy, and they laid hands on the Apostles and put them in the public place of custody.

Miraculously, the Apostles were able to escape from the prison and were to be found teaching and instructing others in the Temple. They were then taken, without violence, to the Religious Authorities known as the Sanhedrin. The Christian community is depicted as creating 'no small stir' among the people and there was a very real fear of unrest.

> But a certain man rose in the Sanhedrin, a Pharisee named Gamaliel, a Law Teacher esteemed by all the people, and gave the command to put the men outside for a little while.
> And he said to them: men of Israel! Pay attention to yourselves as to what you intend to do respecting these men.
> For instance, before these days Theudas rose, saying he himself was somebody, and a number of men, about four hundred, joined his party. But he was done away with, and all those who were obeying him were dispersed and it came to nothing.
> After him Judas the Galilean rose in the days of the registration, and he drew off people after him. And yet that man perished, and all those who were obeying him were scattered abroad.
> And so, under the present circumstances, I say to you: do not meddle with these men, but let them alone; because if this

scheme or this work is from men, it will be overthrown. But if it is from God you will not be able to overthrow them; otherwise, you may perhaps be found fighters actually against God (9).

As the God Process unfolds there is the gradual awakening of the Rational Mind. This is also the evolution of the Human Race, by means of which the Destiny of the Godhead is brought to fruition.

There must be Change; yet too much Change can be counter-productive, indeed too much Change, too quickly, can produce a very powerful reaction. Ancient Egypt was to experience this at first hand.

In the Eighteenth Dynasty (10), the religious life of Egypt, which was centred on Thebes, was rocked to its very foundations.

Amenophis IV, who was clearly a forceful individual in his own right, presided over an administration at the height of its power. In the second year of his reign, he abruptly announced that he was replacing Ra by a Sun-god in a new form. This was the Aten, always portrayed as the actual disk of the Sun with its rays coming down to earth. If Amenophis had simply promoted the Aten among the other traditional Egyptian gods, there might have been little trouble, but he decided on nothing less than the forceful imposition of the Aten and the complete eradication of the old gods.

In an astonishingly provocative act, the King constructed a major new Temple to the Aten in Thebes itself. It must have aroused ferocious opposition. Two years later the King took the more ambitious but less foolhardy course of building a new capital downstream on the east bank of the river, at an uninhabited site where the rays of the rising Sun broke through a cliff. It was to be called Akhetaten (11), and when he moved there Amenophis gave himself a new name, Akhenaten (12). His wife, Queen Nefertiti, who had been associated with the New Cult in Thebes, also took a new title, Nefernefruaten (13). She was given a prominent role in the Cult of the Aten, standing alongside the King himself in many of the ceremonies.

Fundamental to the reforms must have been the desire to focus attention away from the Theban Priesthood to the person of the King, himself. To achieve this, Akhenaten revived the old idea that an individual's afterlife depended on his loyalty to the King, who was the sole intermediary between the Human Race and the Aten.

The impact of Akhenaten's Reforms was profound. In order to finance his building at Akhetaten (normally known by its modern name el-Amarna) and to destroy rival gods, many Temples were closed down and their wealth confiscated in the King's name. This caused massive disruption to the economy (14).

The Cult of the Aten was not sufficient for people; because of this it was always going to be very unlikely that people would cling to the new god. It is said that even those workmen who built Akhetaten continued to worship the more traditional gods of Egypt.

Akenaten's son-in-law, Smenkhkare, was to succeed Akhenaten but, unfortunately, Smenkhkare died within a few months. This meant that the throne would be ascended by Tutankhamun (15) who was no more than the tender age of nine. Tutankhamun had formerly been known as Tutankhaten, "the living image of the Aten".

III

In Ancient Egypt, after the unfortunate circumstances arising from the enforced *Cult of the Aten*, circumstances which had led to the economic exhaustion of Egypt, there was a burning desire to return to more conservative ways and for the restoration of harmony. The principal way in which this happened was the return, or reinstatement, of those beliefs pertaining to *the sacred ibis*.

Those alive at the time who sought to regulate Egypt's bearings by means of theological reform were motivated by the recognition of certain truths. The first of these was in relation to the Sun, itself.

No one would ever dare to deny the importance of the Sun in the life of the Human Race. It was obvious to all concerned that without the Sun, life would be impossible. As a Deity, the Sun was able to become the focus of

Creeds which expressed *the universal*; the Sun made life possible and it *freely* shed its light on all, irrespective of Nation, Creed or Colour. As a specifically unifying symbol it was beyond compare.

While recognising the importance of the Sun we must not be beguiled into thinking that the existence of the Sun is all there is to it; there was the Nile, for example. Herodotus, the great historian from Antiquity, maintained that "Egypt was the gift of the Nile". We certainly need sunlight to make life possible but we also need water to sustain it (16).

It may be possible that the purpose of the opening chapter of the Bible is the intention of drawing the reader away from Sun-worship (17). The first book of the Bible, *The Book of Genesis*, begins by stating:

> In the beginning God created the heavens and the Earth. Now the Earth proved to be formless and waste and there was darkness upon the surface of the watery deep; and God's active force was moving to and fro over the surface of the waters.

Starlight appeared and, after this, there was the appearance of dry land, which was to be referred to as Earth. Whilst the expanse of the waters became seas, on the land grass, vegetation and fruit trees appeared.

As the development takes place it is not until the sixteenth verse of the first chapter of *The Book of Genesis* that:

> God proceeded to make two great luminaries, the greater luminary for dominating the day and the lesser luminary for dominating the night, and also the stars. Thus God put them in the expanse of the heavens to shine upon the Earth and to dominate by day and by night and to make a division between the light and the darkness.

Perhaps there is an attempt here to downplay the importance of the Sun and there are good reasons for this. Those prophetic communities which have existed from immemorial Antiquity have been trying to bring Humanity to the stage whereby the Human Race can be *initiated* into *The Mysteries*.

Plato was adamant that "life on earth is but a passing episode"; Plato would obviously be talking from the point of view of one with considerable insight, for he had already been initiated into *The Mysteries*.

Plato would have been motivated by the Knowledge that the purpose of life is the unfolding of the Predisposition of God to be God. During this Unfolding or Evolution of the Predisposition of God to be God, there is a Human *stage*, the Destiny of God being dependent upon the Human Race, the Racial Memory of the Original Godhead, the Divine Identity awaiting completion.

Religion exists to unite people, to provide them with Instruction suitable enough to have a civilising influence upon people. The author (John Houston) is still mesmerised by the fact that there have existed for millennia communities whose task it is to guide the Human Race on an altruistic path. Non-violence, the Oneness of the Human Race, indeed the Oneness of all life and a morality built upon respect are proclaimed as fundamental to all true Religion all over the planet.

As the Human Race is guided along the Path of Illumination as to the reason *why* the Human Race exists, there is no symbol more potent than that of *the sacred ibis*.

Among other places, the sacred ibis is to be found living among the reeds which grow by the banks of the Nile. It is by means of these reeds that the ibis is able to manufacture papyrus. Once created the sacred ibis intuitively begins to record the Divine Word for the sake of *revealing* the Mind of God to Humanity.

In the communication from the sacred ibis there was the illumination brought about by the Light of the Mind. Here we are reminded of Apollo whose light shone in order to disperse that Darkness which some Mystics still refer to as *Ahriman*.

The Light of Apollo is Life, Itself. The sacred ibis operated in such a way as to communicate in relation to guidance the Human Race requires to reach a level of Self-Knowledge.

Darkness will be dispelled. Just as the Sun rises in the morning by means of those 'steads of the brave Helios', so the Light of the Mind must shine to dispel the Darkness of Ignorance, wherever possible.

> The Egyptians mourned the loss of the life-giving Sun over the Western horizon. It is said that Re commanded Thoth to provide light in the Sun's absence, and the Moon was thus formed. As a lunar Deity Thoth was naturally associated with Time and the Calendar.

Thoth was worshiped in ibis or baboon form, and often depicted holding a reed pen. He was scribe to the gods, and also official recorder at the Weighing of the Heart ceremony. Thoth was also the god of Wisdom. He was believed to have devised hieroglyphic writings, and to have written forty-two books containing the wisdom of the entire world (18).

IV

It is no exaggeration to assert that we are now living at the most crucial stage in the development of Human Culture. We stand at a crossroads.

We are now in the cusp between two Ages. The Old World Order is beginning to collapse as it should. It has served its purpose. Now it will be replaced as the Old Order recedes into History.

As the Old Order collapses and we enter upon 'the mass extinction event' with millions of people being wiped out, leadership will appear to guide through troubled waters those who may enter the Kingdom. As has been the case from Antiquity it will be the sacred ibis which will provide guidance for those who will inherit the Kingdom.

The mass extinction event will be a judgement on the way that Human communities have been organized. Judgement will fall upon us because we have allowed the Destiny of the Human Race to fall into the hands of mass-merchandisers and bankers. Lacking the insight which can only be provided by such as the Brahmins, the controllers and manipulators who presently govern us do so "without any ambition to protect the sufferers". Their main concern is their own self-advancement.

The guidance required by the Human Race will be supplied by the One who has guided the Human Race this far. As the Divine Pharaoh, he will have the final say in who will be able to enter the Kingdom of God.

The Human Race must undergo the Day of Judgement. Those who enter the Kingdom will have to possess those attributes which the Great Shepherd, the Divine Pharaoh, requires of Human beings; at the very least they would need to be civilised.

Here we are reminded of a passage from the Writings of Plato:

Hermes asked Zeus how he should impart Justice and Reverence among men: Should he distribute them as the Arts are distributed; that is to say, to a favoured few only, one skilled individual having enough of Medicine or of any other Art for the many unskilled ones? "Shall this be the manner in which I am to distribute Justice and Reverence among men, or shall I give them to all?"

"To all," said Zeus.

"I should like them all to have a share; for cities cannot exist, if only a few share in the Virtues, as in the Arts. And further, make a law by my order, that he who has no part in Justice and Reverence shall be put to death, for he is a plague on the State" (19).

We need to see the appearance of a New World Order which will lay the foundations for a sustainable economic system which will take the Human Race through the impending tribulation and on, into the future, and the Realisation of Destiny.

As the most powerful nation on Earth, the United States of America, the natural successor to the British Empire, will have a pivotal influence on the unfolding of Human Destiny.

The author (John Houston) believes that as the present system collapses there will be the coming together of the English-speaking nations to create a New World Order. Although it is true to say that, in the English-speaking world, not all the problems have been solved they are, nonetheless, like a guiding light unto the rest of Humanity because of their freedoms, their liberality, their education and unrivalled creativity.

In the future, any coalition of nations on Earth united for the betterment of our likelihood of survival will be dependent to a considerable extent upon the English-speaking nations. The importance that an alliance of the English-speaking nations would be able to exert is unquantifiable. This has been alluded to elsewhere.

When asked in 1898 to name a defining factor in recent history, the German Chancellor Bismarck replied, "North America speaks English". To linguist Nicholas Ostler, that anecdote reveals how "far more than princes, states or economies, it is language-communities who are the real players in world history". In this engrossing and original narrative, Ostler gives us five millennia of world history as seen through "the Empires of the Word".

We can trace the birth of literacy to the 'three sisters', Sumerian, Akkadian and Aramaic, in the Fertile Crescent of the late fourth millennium BC. Like empires, languages can rise and fall, but why did Egyptian fall out of favour before the advance of Arabic, while Chinese resisted over 2000 years of invasions? Languages must evolve, and Ostler explains how an insistence on linguistic purity can be linked to the death of Ancient Greek as a spoken language. In contrast, English is a chameleon. It was first transformed by the Normans, then 300 years later new economic realities in the wake of the Black Death led to the rise of the vernacular. In the following centuries, from its foothold in just one American colony in 1586, English grew to become the *lingua franca* of the world (20).

With the dawning of the New Age, there will be birth pangs. One Age will wither and die whereas, in its stead, there will be something better for us.

It is about the Realisation of Destiny, about the Appearance of 'the One amongst the many'. This is the Ultimate Ancestor intent upon the creation of a means of existence which will permit the Ultimate Ancestor to exist *as* God. The Ultimate Ancestor does this within the context of the unfolding of Predisposition.

A Kingdom will appear on Earth. It will arise from a radical union of the English-speaking nations, with others.

The Kingdom of God will be built upon the English language and, in terms of belief, it will go beyond Protestantism, this being possible because of the Incarnation of the Great Shepherd who will guide the Human Race into the future.

Every eye will see him and every knee shall bow. This will mean the end of the Human stage of evolution.

The Human Race will be further deified, enabling them to cross-fertilize with those Beings from the world of the Biblical Angels who are intent upon creating a home for themselves on Earth.

The Human Race will be assimilated into their Greater Life which is also the Life of God.

NOTES

(1)   The Christian community often refer to the Godhead as Father, Son and Holy Ghost, denoting the existence of a *Relationship* of Godhead. From the Hindus we have something similar with the Hindus referring to the Godhead of Brahma, Vishnu and Shiva.

(2)   Jesus of Nazareth, in Christian Tradition, is often referred to as 'Alpha and Omega, the Beginning and the End' of everything. As it happens, the first letter of the Greek Alphabet is Alpha, whereas the final letter of the Greek Alphabet is Omega.

(3)   Thoth of the ibis beak is depicted as being 'the arbiter of all conflicts'.

(4)   Lord Krishna renders devotional service to the Human Race, as the means of the Realisation of the Destiny of the Godhead, by *eliminating unwanted population.*

   In *The Bhagavad Gita*, chapter 3, verse 24 we read:

   If I did not perform prescribed duties, all these worlds would be put to ruination. I would be the cause of creating unwanted population, and I would thereby destroy the peace of all living beings.

(5)   Born in Corning, New York in 1883 and educated at Claverach College, Margaret Louise Higgins was a trained nurse.

   In 1902 she married William Sanger; in 1914 she published *The Woman Rebel*, a radical feminist magazine; in 1916, she established in Brooklyn, New York City, America's first Birth-Control Clinic, in consequence of which she was to be imprisoned.

(6)   Edwin Black, *War Against the Weak. Eugenics and America's Campaign to Create a Master Race.* Published by *Thunder's Mouth Press*, New York. First Paperback Edition of October 2004. See page 12.

   Pertaining to Herbert Spencer 1820-1903, the English revolutionary philosopher, we read:

In the 1850s, agnostic English philosopher Herbert Spencer published *Social Statics*, asserting that Man and Society, in truth, followed the laws of cold science, not the will of a caring, Almighty God. Spencer popularised a powerful new term: survival of the fittest. He declared that Man and Society were evolving according to their inherited nature. Through evolution, "the fittest" would naturally continue to perfect Society. And "the unfit" would naturally become more impoverished, less educated and ultimately die off as well they should. Indeed, Spencer saw the misery and starvation of the pauper classes as an inevitable decree of a "far-seeing benevolence", that is, the Laws of Nature. He unambiguously insisted, "the whole effort of Nature is to get rid of such, and to make room for better ... If they are not sufficiently complete to live, they die, and it is best that they should die".

(7) as (6) above. See page 129.

(8) Henry Fairfield Osborn (1857-1935) was born in Fairfield, Connecticut.
     He studied at Princeton and became Professor of Zoology at Columbia University and concurrently Curator of Vertebrate Palaeontology at the American Museum of Natural History.

(9) The Acts of the Apostles, Chapter 5, verses 34-39.

(10) In Ancient Egypt, the Eighteenth Dynasty lasted from 1550 BC until 1307 BC.
      It was founded by Ahmose in 1550 BC and ended in 1307 BC with the death of Haremhab.

(11) This means 'Horizon of the Sun god'.

(12) The name means 'Agreeable to the Aten'.

(13) The meaning of the name is 'Fair is the goddess of the Aten'.

(14) Charles Freeman. *Ancient Egypt.* Advisory Editor: John D. Ray. Published by Angus Books Limited, London in 2005. From the chapter, *The Eternal Kingdom.* See page 52.

(15) The name means 'living image of Amun'.

(16) There is divergence among Religions which give rise to different systems of belief; some have attributed more importance to the Sun. There is a general acceptance that, as was the case with Zoroaster, Sun-worship was the prime motivator in the religious experience of the Human Race.

The *Cult of Isis* and *The Cult of Mary*, which became synonymous during the time of the Roman Empire, were about the veneration of the Earth Mother.

(17) The Bible, as we know it, is a manifestation of the Royal Lie propagated by the Vatican. For Rome, any veneration of the Sun or the Moon would have been viewed as idolatrous, therefore forbidden.

In the opinion of the author (John Houston) there would have been a more far-reaching motive in undermining the Sun, the Moon and the Stars; the Vatican would want to undermine belief in Astrology.

Rome's aim was to produce a Religion which created a population psychologically dependent upon the Religion of Rome and the Priesthood as the *sole* means of salvation.

For *The Cult of Jesus Christ*, the future could not be concerned with Astrology because the keys of the future Kingdom belonged to the Vatican, with the Vatican being God's *sole* representative.

(18) R. Hamilton, *Ancient Egypt. Kingdom of the Pharaohs.* Published by Paragon Books in 2006. From the sixth chapter, *The Gods*, page 248f.

(19) *The Dialogues of Plato.* Great Books of the Modern World. Mortimer J. Adler, Editor in Chief. *The Seventh Letter.* Translated by J. Harward. *The Encyclopaedia Britannica, Inc.* 1996 printing. From *The Protagoras*, page 44.

(20) This comes from an introduction to the book, *Empires of the Word*, by linguist Nicholas Ostler. The book is to be published by *The Folio Society*, London in 2010.

About John Houston

I was born on 26 July 1950 in the Southern General hospital in the South of Glasgow, Scotland's largest city.

On that day my father had gone to work in the shipyard as usual. Not long after he had gone to work my mother started to have contractions. In due course she was taken by ambulance to hospital.

The very first thing I remember saying to my mother when still very young was that I had lived before. Who I had been or where I had lived remained a mystery to me; I was able to recount experiences which I had had whilst *out of the body*.

Psychologically speaking it was a dream-like state, as though I were a *neuron of memory*; then I remember beginning to transcend by physical form and looking out of my eyes. I heard a voice saying to me "this is your next task". I was eight months old. My mother was changing my clothes. This is John Houston's first experience.

Years passed. I lived my life in expectation of meeting people whom I had known before. Then when I was eight years old and walking to primary school in the area of Castlemilk in Glasgow, *the vision came to me*. Right there and right then I realised that there was going to be a great transition for the Human Race. It was because of *the necessity* of this transition that I had come here *to the Earth* because I would be involved in this transition. That was what my life would entail.

One year later, while in a class at Netherton Primary, I realised that I would have to be transformed. It was as though I was looking down on myself from a distance. I could see my crown chakra. It was being activated. I realised that I would have to be transformed, like a butterfly emerging from a chrysalis. How I was then was one thing; yet how I was then was not the way I truly was for there was a power within me which demanded an awakening *within* me and *of* me.

I experienced a great restlessness during adolescence, but I had seen the vision and I was thereby empowered to deal with anything that came my way.

It wasn't until early January 1980 that things really started to happen again. I saw the thousand-petalled lotus of Krishna and, thereafter, the writings began *to come to me*. I wrote them down as I was inspired to do.

I didn't go looking for this Truth or this Knowledge, because it came to me.

I am who I am and I will be who I will be.